Finding Meaning with Mandalas:
A Therapist's Guide to Creating Mandalas with Children

© 2015 Tracy Turner-Bumberry
Turner Phrase Publishing LLC
Saint Charles, Missouri

All rights reserved. No part of this book may be reproduced, stored in a retrieval system, or transmitted, in any form or by any means, electronic, mechanical, photo copying, microfilming, recording, or otherwise, without written permission of the author.

Worksheets and handouts may be reproduced only within the confines of the use with clients. This limited permission does not grant other rights, nor does it give permission for commercial, resale, syndication or any other use not contained above. Another use or reproduction is a violation of international laws and is forbidden without express written permission from the author.

ISBN: 978-0-9964199-1-8

Correspondence regarding this book:

Tracy Turner-Bumberry LPC, RPT-S, CAS
Email: tracy@kscounselingstl.com
www.kscounselingstl.com
Facebook Page: KS Counseling

IN MEMORY OF

LIAM CARTER

October 31, 2000 - March 2, 2015

"May the wind under your wings bear you where the sun sails and the moon walks."
J.R.R. Tolkien, The Hobbit

Contents

Foreword by Dr. Robert Jason Grant

Preface

1	Introduction	1
2	History of Mandalas	4
3	Mandala Use in Early Psychotherapy	14
4	Shapes in Art and Psychotherapy	21
5	Color Use in Art and Psychotherapy	33
6	Current Research on Using Mandalas in Psychotherapy	41
7	Guidelines for Mandala Use in Psychotherapy	47
8	Mandala Interventions to Use with Children	54
9	Final Thoughts	151
	References	153

Foreword

Several years ago I walked into a Missouri Association for Play Therapy training and sat down beside Tracy Turner-Bumberry. We began a conversation, and I was instantly drawn to her wisdom, creativity, and love for play therapy and working with children. That was the beginning of our professional relationship and friendship. I have had the opportunity to work with Tracy on several projects since our initial meeting, and I can happily say that my instinct about the quality of her as a person and as a professional have held solid.

Tracy's ownership and operation of KS Counseling Clinic in St. Charles, Missouri is only the beginning of her professional reach. Tracy is a Registered Play Therapist Supervisor and a Certified AutPlay Therapy Provider. For several years she has worked in the therapeutic environment with children and adolescents dealing with a variety of diagnoses and struggles. Her reputation as a therapist in the St. Louis area and greater state of Missouri is exceptional. She is regularly invited to speak and present trainings, as she is a highly sought after and experienced trainer. I have hosted play therapy workshops presented by Tracy, and have personally witnessed just how engaging and effective she is as a trainer. This is why I recently asked Tracy to present at the first AutPlay Therapy Conference. I knew that the first AutPlay Conference had to be excellent in order to bring participants back and grow the event. With this realization in mind, Tracy was at the top of my list, and the first professional I invited to present.

As I write this foreword I am reminded of a training I asked Tracy to facilitate at my training clinic; I believe the title was "Play Therapy Interventions to Reduce Anxiety and Stress". As I sat in the training listening and participating in several stress reducing, mindfulness interventions, I had no idea how much these approaches, and the engaging process that Tracy used to present the approaches, would impact my personal life. To this day, I am not only teaching the mindful stress reducing strategies that I learned to the children that I work with, but also implementing them in my own life. Little did I know at the time of her training that I would be learning and implementing a mindfulness approach in my own personal life that has greatly helped reduce my own anxiety and stress levels.

The professional and personal learning obtained from attending one of Tracy's trainings should have been no surprise to me. This speaks to the level of proficiency she has as a therapist, trainer, and overall professional in the field of therapeutically working with children and adolescents. Tracy's most recent professional endeavor, the writing and publication of *Finding Meaning* with *Mandalas: A Therapist's Guide to Creating Mandalas with Children,* aligns with Tracy's professional orientations and her creative, transforming, and engaging character. It is hard for me to imagine a more qualified person to write this book. Readers should rest assured that Tracy's professional knowledge, practical application, and her personal essence are greatly present on each page of this important publication. Readers should also rest assured that Tracy's work in *Finding Meaning with Mandalas* (as in everything she does) is grounded in research and thoughtful application for the general practitioner.

When someone asks me to write a foreword for their upcoming book and my immediate response is "Yes," "Absolutely," or "I would love to," that is a wonderful feeling. I am honored to write this foreword and support the work that Tracy has done in *Finding Meaning with Mandalas*. I am excited about the growth and discovery readers are sure to gain from this book and the significant contribution it brings to using mandalas in therapeutic work with children.

Robert Jason Grant Ed.D
Author, AutPlay Therapy Handbook

Preface

One of my earliest memories is the happiness I felt when coloring a picture out of a brand new coloring book. My sister and I especially enjoyed a game we created in which we would choose an object from the coloring page, close our eyes, blindly pick a color, and then color that object our chosen color. Did we ever have wild looking finished products back then! As we grew older, we became thrilled with the new graphic coloring books, filled with images of patterns to brightly color. Several of these books included beautiful circular pictures, created with symmetrical shapes, and a mesmerizing, eye-catching center. Little did I know then that I was coloring my first mandala.

As a Registered Play Therapist Supervisor, I work with a variety of child and teen clients where play is always the theme. I have a large sand tray in my office, and I often invite clients to create a "sand picture" using the miniatures on my shelves. I began noticing that some of my clients chose to make circular works of art with the miniatures, which reminded me of the mandalas I originally colored. These clients' creations seemed to enhance their relaxation during the session, and seemed to always be constructed spontaneously. While processing the finished product with the client, I noticed the client was often unaware that a circular design had been created. I then began using mandala works of art as a directive intervention and continued to discover the great healing they created. After documenting many of these interventions, I decided a book was in order.

This book is written for any therapist who prefers to use art and/or play therapy techniques to enhance the client session. I believe that art and play are paramount when working with any child, and that all adults could benefit from becoming more childlike.

This book will first describe what a mandala is, the cultural references of mandalas throughout time, and the significance of shapes and colors used when creating mandalas. The book also discusses the therapeutic uses of mandalas in early therapy, and some current research as to the effectiveness of mandala creation. The bulk of the book, however will be the instruction of fifty mandala interventions, complete with pictures, that can be done with clients of any age, culture or diagnosis.

I would like to acknowledge the many people who have been a continuous source of inspiration to me, not only during writing, but throughout my life: my parents Rich and Joyce Turner, siblings Anne Perry and Rick Turner, my husband Michael Bumberry, daughter Savannah Turner and my fur children Ozzy and Louie. Special recognition goes to my friend Eileen Heidenheimer who not only provided me with many books on the subject of mandalas, but also gave me constant encouragement to help me proceed on this path. I am also indebted to Christy Ratliff-Hayes who took on the painstaking task of editing this book, which we both called "my baby". Her wisdom and attention to detail has been of great benefit. Professionally, I have to thank my wonderful KS Counseling team, and Dr. Robert Jason Grant, my personal mentor. Finally I wish to thank my spiritual sangha at Mid America Buddhist Association for helping me walk the path of mindfulness in this ever chaotic world.

Most importantly, I wish to share my love and gratitude to each and every client who has been placed in my care. You are all a constant source of strength and inspiration, and I am honored to be a part of your lives.

Whomever I have forgotten; you may have been forgotten in my head, but never in my heart.

-Tracy Turner-Bumberry, April 2015

Chapter 1

Introduction

"Each person's life is like a mandala-a vast, limitless circle. We stand in the center of our own circle, and everything we see, hear and think forms the mandala of our life."
-Pema Chodron, *Living Beautifully with Uncertainty and Change*

For those with previous knowledge and experience in mandalas, this quote about these works of art and beauty rings true. A mandala is indeed a vast, limitless circle, with a clearly defined center, often representing our own life journey. Mandalas have been mystical and artistic vehicles for divine purpose, meditation support, and as great examples of works of art. Yet others may be asking what exactly is a mandala, and moreover, how can it be used in a client therapy session? The beauty and magical quality of a mandala are wonderful tools to use with all ages in all stages of therapy, and this book will detail how this can be implemented.

To begin at the very beginning, it is important to define what a mandala is for anyone who is new to the subject, or for anyone who may need a refresher. The word "mandala" comes from the ancient Indian language of Sanskrit and is loosely translated to mean a "circle" or "orb". In Hindu and Buddhist practices, mandalas would be defined as deeply spiritual symbols representing the universe. These symbols were considered sacred art, and constructed to allow for deeper meditation and awakening, as well as completed during spiritual rituals.

Early psychoanalysts, most notably Carl Jung, would define a mandala as a universal archetype or symbol in a dream, in which the dreamer could create a mandala artistically when awake. He believed that mandalas represented the dreamer's search for completeness, and creating mandala artwork could aid in this search.

Whatever definition is used, a mandala is a mystical and personal tool to help achieve growth within even our youngest clients. This book is a guide to help therapy professionals use mandalas in a variety of interventions. We begin with a more in-depth look at the history and uses of mandalas both throughout time and various regions of the world. Special attention will then be focused on the early use of mandalas in psychotherapy, in particular the contributions of psychoanalyst Carl Jung. Next, the symbolism of particular shapes and colors in both art and in therapy settings will be explored. This will allow the therapist to fully see and process the choices of shapes and colors a client may use when creating mandalas. Art therapy has provided a great deal of research in this area, which is crucial for all therapists to understand, especially when working with mandala works of art.

The latter sections hold the greatest value to therapists working with clients of all ages, especially children. In-depth explanation of how to conduct a mandala intervention with a client, as well as how to process the finished art work will be detailed. Conducting and processing a mandala session is paramount for therapists to know in order for the client to fully benefit from this intervention. Detailed steps are given on how to accomplish this, as well as a script for those who feel more comfortable having the dialogue pre-written. Finally, this book provides fifty mandala interventions that can be used for clients of any age to provide significant meaning and understanding to both the therapist and the client.

For those therapists who are ready to have meaningful and dynamic art sessions with their clients, as well as a reservoir of interventions to immediately use during their sessions, this book will highlight just that. It may also hold a dual purpose of allowing you, the therapist, to enhance your own self-care and creativity by completing your own personal mandala artwork. As I often remind the workshop participants who attend my trainings, it is only through taking care of ourselves that we can truly take care of our clients. Peace to all reading this, and let's begin our journey!

Chapter 2

History of Mandalas

"As body is to the soul and oil is to the lamp, a yantra is to the deity"
-Kularnava Tantra (Chap., v 86)

There is a long and storied tradition in the usage of mandalas throughout the world. These symbols have been featured in religious ceremonies, created within art and architecture, and availed as a deep and profound meditation tool. One only has to view stained glass windows in a Gothic church, or attend a museum of ancient art to notice the multiple uses mandalas have held throughout time. Although many cultures and countries have used mandalas in their practices, this chapter will focus on four primary religious/spiritual cultures in which mandala creation was the most prolific. The Hindu, Tibetan Buddhist, Native American and Christian cultures each have a beautiful and spiritual way in which mandalas were used to heighten personal development. Although the techniques may differ, it is interesting to notice how all of these cultures used, and continue to use, mandalas to promote a greater sense of peace and stability within the creator and viewer. This suggests the idea of a *collective unconscious* that views circles as a deep symbol of life itself and the ultimate wholeness of the individual. Discerning the powerful benefits of creating mandalas in the therapy session will be clearer after investigating various cultural perspectives on mandala use.

The Hindu Yantra

The Sanskrit word for a mandala is *yantra*, literally meaning "a device for holding or fastening". The first examples of yantras are found as early as 3000 B.C.E. The Harappan Culture (2,500-1,600 BCE), in the Indus River Valley of India was one of the world's first great civilizations, complete with a writing system, a city center and a detailed economic and social structure. Remains found from the Harappan Culture show seals with designs that strongly resemble yantras (Avalon, 2007).

The yantra is a powerful, vital, sacred symbol, believed to hold the energy and life force of an element, form, or concept. The traditional yantras were discovered through revelation by spiritual masters, known as gurus. Only a guru could reveal a yantra to the world. They were typically drawn on paper or engraved onto metal. They could also be found designed on floors and used in architecture. In later use, yantras were applied as a highly efficient tool for deeper states of meditation (Khanna, 1979).

Yantras are geometric compositions which consist of abstract symbols. All yantras have a *bindu* (literally meaning "dot") in the middle, which is known as the sacred center. The bindu is a symbol of the "one" in complete wholeness; the point of origin of all. During meditation, the focus is on the bindu, which leads to greater spiritual contemplation. Yantras also consist of triangles, circles, squares, and lines, each having their own spiritual significance (The significance of symbols will later be discussed in Chapter 4). Four T-shaped portals, one at each of the four cardinal directions, are also the hallmark of yantra construction. These four doors are seen as cosmic doors in which the meditator symbolically enters (Khanna, 1979).

A unique quality of yantras is the sound symbol associated with them. This sound symbol is known as a *mantra*, and each yantra has its own mantra. A mantra is a thought, word, sound or phrase that protects and guides. It means to transcend the mind (Khanna, 1979). A well known mantra in Hinduism is *om*. The most important mantra symbol is found in the center of the yantra, with other important symbols radiating outwards of the creation. A practitioner meditating on a yantra, while also focusing on the sound of the mantra is believed to achieve great spiritual enlightenment (Khanna, 1979).

Yantras are continued to be used in modern day Tantric Hinduism, in which rituals and spiritual practice are incorporated to achieve liberation from ignorance in an effort to gain enlightenment. Directions for the correct use of the yantra include hanging the yantra on a wall facing north or east, while placing the yantra at eye level based on one's meditation posture. The meditator would then begin to meditate, focusing on the bindu, while calmly breathing in and out. Using the yantra as a meditative aid has been seen to strengthen the meditation experience, and aids in self-calming and mindfulness (Avalon, 2007).

The Sri Yantra, known as the most famous Hindu Yantra

The Tibetan Buddhist Mandala

Although mandalas have been discovered in many Buddhist traditions, it is the Tibetan tradition in which the mandala holds the most sacred significance. The Tibetan word for mandala is *kyilkhor,* which means "center and surrounding environment" (Bryant, 1994). It is believed in the Tibetan tradition that when one contemplates the mandala, one could attain an enlightened state of mind. An enlightened mind is a mind released of any craving or aversion, filled with loving kindness, compassion, wisdom and altruistic joy.

Mandalas are extensively used during tantric practice; it is important to note the Tibetan Buddhist tradition regards the tantras as the highest form of practice. Tantric practices involve ritual and spiritual experiences in which to attain inner enlightenment. Practitioners maintain an ethical lifestyle while working inwardly towards wisdom (Bryant, 1994). A mandala is one tool used to achieve this state of enlightenment. It is believed that each person has a unique spiritual experience upon seeing the mandala for the first time. A person is said to "enter the mandala" when he or she first sees the mandala and internalizes this experience.

The Kalachakra Initiation is one ritual which directly uses the mandala in the practice. Kalachakra means "Wheel of Time", and is the name of one of the Buddhist deities. This deity represents certain aspects of the enlightened mind. The Kalachakra is an ancient teaching which for years was kept as a secret doctrine; only recently has the meaning become more accessible. The Fourteenth Dalai Lama (the spiritual leader of Tibetan Buddhism) confers the Kalachakra Initiation a number of times throughout the world. One part of this twelve day initiation is the creation of the Kalachakra Sand Mandala. This mandala is a complex and colorful design which is a pictorial manifestation of the Kalachakra . Each component within this mandala is a symbol representing an aspect of the teaching (Bryant, 1994). The mandala is created out of sand by several monks, and takes weeks to complete. As a symbol of the impermanence of life, the mandala is dismantled after the viewing.

Any mandala can be used as a spiritual aid to meditation by the novice practitioner. A mandala can be drawn, painted, or made out of particles, such as sand or stones. Creating a mandala can also be a helpful tool for concentration and relaxation.

Monks working on a Kalachakra Sand Mandala-Photo by Kim Yanoshik

The Christian Mandala

One may not think of the Christian tradition when first considering mandala creation, yet mandalas have been used extensively in Christianity. Stained glass windows, official seals, and religious paintings are but a few examples using the symbolism and design of a mandala. One rarely heard of Christian figure who used mandalas in her spiritual life was Hildegard of Bingen, a 12th century German writer, composer, philosopher, artist, and

Benedictine abbess. From a very young age Hildegard had deep religious visions and was sent to live in a monastery at the young age of eight. She expressed that these visions were all seen through the "light of God" and were experienced through all five of her senses. She was given a divine message to write all that she saw, heard and felt during these visions, which prompted her writing and artwork. She wrote extensively, and at the age of forty-two, in the approximate year 1135, Hildegard began to create beautiful art through her visions (Flanagan, 1999). These works of art unmistakably resemble the mandala. Her mandalas spoke of the humanity in the universe, the God-like nature within all, and the inter-connectedness of all of God's creatures (Flanagan, 1999). For a woman over 850 years ago to express these views of humanity, cosmic healing and visionary spirituality, was rare indeed! Hildegard of Bingen has contributed greatly to the contemplative nature of Christianity that many have yet to discover.

Universal Man, or, Man at the Center of the Universe.
Hildegard of Bingen, *Liber Divinorum Operum*, 1165 (13th-century copy).
Biblioteca Statale, Lucca, Codex Latinum 1942 c. 9.

```
Humanity in the Center of the University-by Hildegard of Bingen
```

Mandalas continue to be used in modern day Christian traditions. Books have been written on the ways mandalas can be created to further strengthen one's relationship with God. Christian mandalas are said to be God-focused and completed while reflecting upon Scripture. It is believed that the Holy Spirit is an integral tool in fueling the creative process. The mandala is seen to be a visual tool in order to achieve deeper awareness, inner transformation, and a stronger relationship with God and His word (Pierce, 2014).

Native American Mandalas

The Native American culture seamlessly regards self, nature and spirituality into daily practice. Although there are hundreds of diverse tribes, the underlying theme within all of the traditions is the idea of community; involving all aspects of the natural world to one's practice is a defining belief (Dare to Discern, 2005). The Native American people did not follow a standard set of written religious doctrine, rather their beliefs stemmed on the sacredness of nature and the respect for all. Mandalas are an essential part of this practice. The circle is seen throughout all of nature, and represents the cycles of life. The Native American word *Wakan-Tanka,* meaning "the great everything" is represented by a circle (Dare to Discern, 2005).

The Native American mandala is used as a spiritual tool to understand the inner workings of one's heart, as well as the interconnectedness to all. The Great Spirit is within, and through harmonizing with every aspect of one's world, it is able to be expressed. The mandala allows for this expression, while heightening one's inner awareness and strength (Tara Mandala, 2014). These mandalas were created using pieces of nature to further enhance one's harmony with the entire earth. The mandalas had meditative uses before, during and after the creation of them.

Some notable Native Americans mandalas which have found their way into mainstream culture are the Dream Catcher and the Labyrinth mandalas. Dream Catcher mandalas were first used by the Sioux Indians. Legend has it that a Sioux mother was having a difficult time getting her child to sleep. She went to the tribe's medicine woman to ask for help. The medicine woman gave her a circle made of willows with spider webs interwoven within the willows. The medicine woman explained that the child was unable to sleep due to horrible nightmares, and that the dream catcher would filter any of the bad dreams, only allowing good dreams to enter (Dare to Discern, 2005). The symbolism of the Dream Catcher mandala shows the power of our own thoughts contributing to the state of our minds. If we attempt to keep scary or anxiety-provoking thoughts from resonating within us, we may have the power to have beautiful dreams within our sleeping and waking moments. This may be a possibility if we continually and gently check in with our thoughts and feelings. The symbolism of the dream catcher also shows the interconnectedness within ourselves, and the need to be aligned with each person, animal and object we encounter to fully understand the Great Spirit within us. Each web shows us how we are not alone, and how others, even the tiniest of creatures, help us on our path to awakening.

Labyrinths are a well-known symbol in the Native American culture of one's personal journey throughout life. The labyrinth has no distinct beginning or ending, symbolizing the eternal nature within us. Labyrinth mandalas help one focus on the individual journey which is taken in a lifetime, with the many paths that can be chosen. It allows for changes to be made, and follows the infinite nature of our true spirit. It helps to see the journey each of us takes to a path of self-discovery. There is no final destination to strive to reach; the moment to moment awareness of the path is key.

One of the most beautiful Native American mandalas that can directly be used in psychology is the Medicine Wheel mandala. It is important to note that the word *medicine* is translated to mean something quite differently in the Native American culture. Medicine in the Native American tradition means the knowledge, insight, and power among all nature that can create deep power within us (Tara Mandala, 2014). The traditional Medicine Wheel mandalas were discovered in the Northwestern United States, and were comprised of a large center stone, with several stones forming quadrants within a circular design. It is assumed that these were used during rituals, celebrations, or even as a calendar. The actual term *Medicine Wheel* mandala came into use in the 1800's to represent the importance of whole balance and harmony within an individual. Illness was viewed as disharmony within, and work was needed to regain harmony with nature, in an effort to restore inner harmony (Gucci, 1961). This mandala consists of the original circle of a traditional mandala, with four quadrants inside of the circle. Each quadrant is a different color, typically black, white, red, and yellow. The quadrants represent the four cardinal directions, the four elements, and particular aspects of nature. The center represents the Self, in relation to the entire universe (Gucci, 1961).

Modern day psychologists can use the Medicine Wheel mandala concept to help clients process where they are in several aspects of their lives. The quadrants can be divided into physical, intellectual, emotional and spiritual health in an effort for clients to realize the importance of harmony within all of these. It has shown to be a useful tool for self exploration and processing how to become whole individuals.

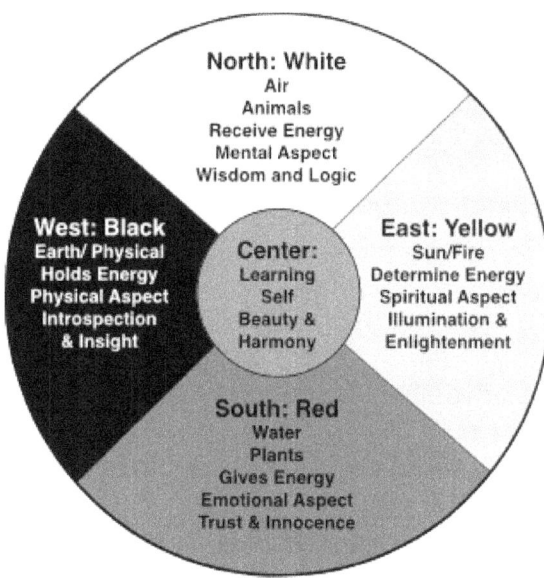

Medicine Wheel Mandala. www.balancedwheelcounseling.com.

Chapter 3

Mandala Use in Early Psychotherapy

"My mandalas were cryptograms concerning the state of the self which was presented to me anew each day...I guarded them like precious pearls...It became increasingly plain to me that the mandala is the center. It is the exponent of all paths. It is the path to the center, to individuation."
 -C.G. Jung "Memories, Dreams, Reflections"

Carl Jung is well-known for being the first therapist to use mandalas in his client sessions. By creating mandalas privately, Jung quickly realized the great power and wisdom he gained from producing these designs. He saw the completed mandala as the *Self*-the totality of the psyche. After creating individual mandalas, Jung began having clients create them as well. Mandala work was of primary importance to Jung, believing that it led to increased self-awareness and understanding.

It is daunting indeed to devote merely one chapter to the great work of Carl Jung. The reader should note that this is a brief summary, merely highlighting Jung's work with mandalas. The assumption has been made that most of the readers have knowledge of Jung and his theory of Individual Psychology, but may not know the specifics of his work with mandalas. For the reader who is looking for more detailed information on the life of Jung and his theories, please look to the reference section for worthy books on the subject. And so, I take a deep breath, and with great reverence to the legacy of Carl Jung, begin.

Jung's Personal Use With Mandalas

Jung created his first mandala in 1916. This was a time for Jung of great introspection and self-awakening. In his book *Memories, Dreams, Reflections,* Jung discusses how in 1913 he began a deep, self-exploration. During this time he wrote, sketched, and painted in a series of black journals, six in all. He explained that this was a time where he purposely and willingly entered deeper states of consciousness in an effort to directly confront his psyche (Jung, 1913). Throughout the years 1913 through 1917, Jung recorded in chronological order his findings to this inner work in great detail. These personal journals are what led to the creation of *The Red Book*, which was largely kept secret until Jung's death in 1961. *The Red Book* only became published and widely distributed in 2009, and shows in great visual beauty the imagination and creativity Jung possessed during his exploration into deeper states of consciousness (Hoeller, 1989).

Jung commented in *Memories, Dreams, Reflections:*

"I sketched every morning in a notebook a small circular drawing, a mandala, which seemed to correspond to my inner situation at the time. With the help of these drawings I could observe my psychic transformations from day to day...My mandalas were cryptograms...in which I saw the self—that is, my whole being—actively at work." (1965: 195-196)

His first mandala was created after writing *Seven Sermons to the Dead*; a collection of seven mystical or *Gnostic* texts privately published, also contained in *The Red Book*. He stated this mandala was inspired by the writing of these sermons, and helped him further explore the concepts of these "discussions with the dead" (Hoeller, 1989). These sermons were privately printed, and Jung would hand the small books out to friends and students.

When *Memories, Dreams, Reflections* was published the sermons were included in the appendix (Hoeller, 1989).

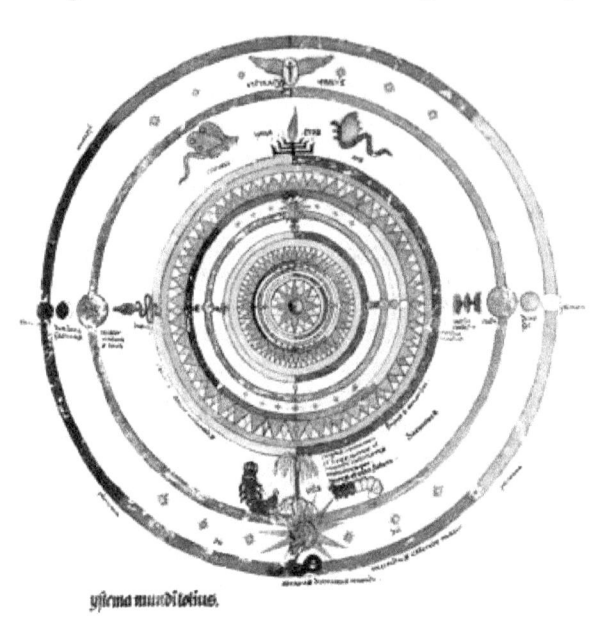

Jung's First Mandala. www.gnosis.org

Jung's Mandala Use With Clients

In Jung's book *Mandala Symbolism*, he further explains the vast, therapeutic benefit of creating mandalas. He believed clients would create mandalas using their own personal, often symbolic, experiences in an effort to express their individuality (Jung, 1992). Whereas Jung's definition of *ego* is comprised of conscious thoughts, his definition of *self* included both conscious and unconscious aspects of individuals. It is through the creation of mandalas that clients will be able to tap into their true Self (Jung, 1992).

Jung believed that both the creation of, and the finished product of a mandala had therapeutic benefits towards clients. He believed that these mandalas needed to be created spontaneously, free from any direction by the therapist. He would often simply ask clients to "make a picture" of previous dreams that were causing them confusion. Jung often noticed the difficulty clients experienced when first creating a mandala, but believed this to be beneficial, since it allowed the unconscious to begin playing a more important role. When observing the mandalas, Jung could see parallels to the creation and the clients' personal struggles and possible solutions, yet always kept these ideas to himself, at least initially. He did not want to influence any future mandalas by suggesting what the current mandala may entail (Jung, 1992).

Jung would help clients who struggled with the creative process simply by telling them not to focus on perfection and to use their "fantasies" to create. He dissuaded them from worrying about the technical details of objects they wished to create. He believed this focus on creativity and fantasy would open the subconscious. This would then guide the client in reaching *individuation,* or the point where life experiences and knowledge of the self leads to a balanced whole (Jung, 1992).

Perhaps Jung's most well-known client when discussing mandala work would be *Miss X*. Miss X was an educated, cultured woman with whom Jung met in the 1920's. She created a series of mandalas which can be easily found online or in several of Jung's books. Her use of mandalas for therapeutic benefit extended over ten years and have provided a great deal of insight into using mandalas in therapy. After her death, the mandalas were given to Jung for further study. Having been given no additional text or explanation from Miss X, Jung was careful to not interpret the pictures too deeply, rather instead focusing on the aspects of individuation throughout the pieces of art (Jung, 1992).

Jung believed that all spontaneous mandalas created by clients held certain archetypal ideas unknown to the creators. Within the diversity of clients, these similar archetypes would be discovered. This further reinforced the idea of a *collective unconscious* to Jung-a similar psychic archetype held within humanity throughout cultures and time. He saw in all mandalas a need for order, balance, and ultimate wholeness of Self (Jung, 1992).

Jung's Psychological Types Explained with a Mandala

Carl Jung was a pioneer in the creation of psychological types to differentiate between behavioral tendencies. Jung spoke of eight different psychological types, highlighted as eight specific and unique patterns for how we perceive, evaluate, understand, and then act based on information presented to us (Jung, 1974). The two main attitudes he discussed were *Extraversion* and *Introversion*; extraversion being one's energy moving and preferring the outside world of people, places, and things; introversion being one's energy preferring thoughts and ideas from within him/herself. Individuals vacillate between the attitudes of extraversion and introversion, yet have a definite preference between the two (Jung, 1992).

Jung also discussed four mental functions within the two umbrellas of *Perceiving* and *Judging* (Jung, 1974). Under the first umbrella of Perceiving, individuals take in information, either through the mental functions of *Sensing* or *Intuition*. Sensing is taking in information primarily through the five senses. Intuition means to make connections and inferences beyond sensory data. Under the second umbrella of Judging, individuals evaluate and then make decisions based on provided data, either through the mental functions of *Thinking* or *Feeling*. Thinking means to evaluate through logic. Feeling is defined by evaluating through feelings and considering what is valuable to the individual (Jung, 1992).

Within each of the four mental functions, the attitude of extraversion or introversion could be attached, which leads to eight psychological types (Jung, 1974). These eight types are:

1. **Extraverted Sensing**- Experiencing externally through senses
2. **Extraverted Intuiting**- Experiencing externally through multiple perspectives
3. **Extraverted Thinking**- Experiencing externally through logic
4. **Extraverted Feeling**- Experiencing externally through emotion
5. **Introverted Sensing**- Experiencing internally through senses
6. **Introverted Intuiting**- Experiencing internally through multiple perspectives
7. **Introverted Thinking**- Experiencing internally through logic
8. **Introverted Feeling**- Experiencing internally through emotion

Modern day psychologists often use circle drawings (what may be called mandalas perhaps?) to help simplify the eight personality types. What better way to honor Jung's theories than with a mandala! Although the mandalas created by Jung and his clients were completely non-directive in nature, the image on the following page gives a glimpse of how a directive mandala may be used. Notice, also, how this mandala strongly resembles the Native American medicine wheel.

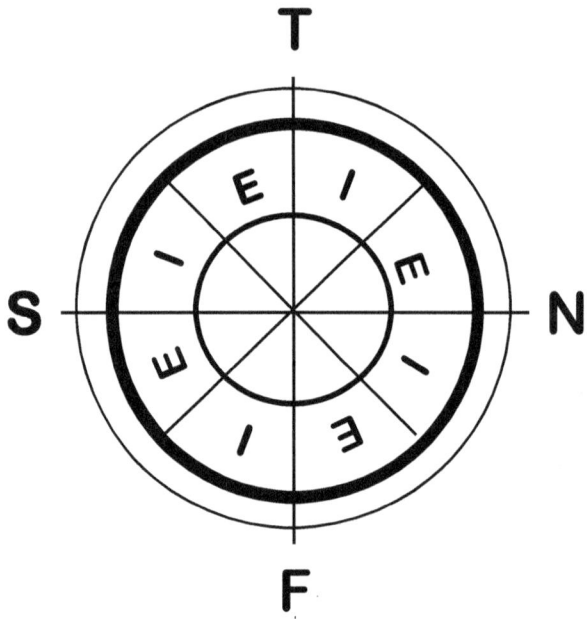

Image of Jung's Eight Personality Types. Used with permission by Katharine D. Myers and MBTItoday.org

T=Thinking, N=Intuiting, F=Feeling, S=Sensing
E=Extraversion, I=Introversion

Chapter 4

Shapes in Art and Psychotherapy

"It is through symbols that man consciously or unconsciously lives, works and has his being."
-Thomas Carlyle

Therapists using mandala interventions during sessions will generally agree that it is the act of creating the mandala that allows for the true healing of the client. Offering the client a sacred space in which to create, free from distraction, interruption or judgement will allow this creativity to blossom. As Jung noted in his writings, processing and making interpretations of the mandala need to be done carefully and individually, with full knowledge that the client is indeed the expert of the creation (Jung, 1992).

Although the various symbols created within the mandala should be processed individually with the client, therapists need to also be aware of certain symbols that appear throughout history and cultures. These symbols show similar meanings among various cultures, revealing a collective archetype within humanity. It is important for the creative arts therapist to have knowledge of some of these universal symbols, especially since they often appear in clients' mandala creations. This does not mean that the clients' interpretation is not key, rather that a grasp of universal symbols can enhance the processing experience.

Geometrical shapes prove to be very powerful, as well as often used, in mandala creations. Art therapists have found that shapes in art can help in the healing of the client (Malchiodi,1999). Continuous repetition of shapes can help produce a rhythm and a flow with the clients that can inspire regulation and calmness within them. Drawing shapes can improve clients' concentration and help clients feel freer to create even more within their artwork (Malchiodi, 1999). Shapes were first learned at a very young age, therefore we have some confidence when creating them. This helps us begin the journey into creating meaningful art. There is additionally a great deal of symbolism within each individual shape which can prove beneficial when processing the artwork.

Many books detail popular symbols in art, and therapists can easily find these resources for a full explanation of symbology. Cultural anthropologist, Angeles Arrien (1998) completed extensive research on over twelve hundred different symbols throughout the world, and discovered five major shapes used in all the cultures she explored. These symbols were found in art and architecture and quite often in mandalas. Due to the primary focus of this book being on mandala interventions, this chapter will detail three symbols found universally and throughout time: the circle, square and triangle. The cross and spiral will briefly be discussed, having been found as two additional shapes used throughout cultures and times, though not as common in mandalas as the circle, square and triangle. There will be additional mention on some other typical shapes I have personally seen often in mandala creations with clients; the heart, the star and lines.

The Circle

The circle is definitively the most used mandala shape, for the mandala itself is in the shape of a circle. A circle is the essence of life itself, and can be found often in the natural world, from stones to birds' nests, flowers to the sun and full moon. A circle has no beginning and no end, which makes for a lovely symbol of the entire cycle of life.

The circle seems to possess an endless, continuous flow, which may be the very reason a mandala is a circle. The circle has significant meaning in religions throughout the world. In Hinduism, the circle is seen as one of the three "root forms" (along with the triangle and square), since a circle is at its most basic closed shape (Khanna, 1979). Although it can be made to be smaller or larger, a circle cannot be reduced down to any other closed, visual shape. This gives it what is called a *primordial* quality, meaning the circle has existed since the beginning of time (or, in some cultures since *beginning-less time*). The circle, in the form of a halo (nimbus), has represented God in Christianity, enlightenment in Buddhism, "The Great Everything" in Native American spirituality, the feminine in Judaism, and magical protection in Wicca.

In psychology, Jung viewed the circle as a great form of protection, sheltering the innermost Self from any outer influences coming into one's core (Jung, 1964). He believed creating a mandala within the protection of this circle allowed for the unconscious to be stimulated and for individuation to occur (Jung, 1992). Art therapists across the world have recognized the circle as an important and meaningful shape. Cathy Malchiodi, a prominent art therapist, discusses in her book, *The Art Therapy Sourcebook* (1998), the special meaning behind the circle. She states how the circle is familiar to humans due to our interactions with circular images in nature from a very young age. The circle helps individuals feel contained, safe, and comfortable. She often has clients who are feeling especially distressed or anxious create artwork within a circle to provide calmness and stability (Malchiodi, 1999).

Cultural anthropologist Angeles Arrien (1998) found that every culture deemed the circle representative of wholeness and unity. The circle represents individuation, where individuals strive for independence, investigation and room within themselves to truly discover who they are. Noticing circles within nature can be a wonderful clue towards the wholeness of the universe. Circles in artwork may symbolize the need for wholeness and safety for expression.

The Triangle

The triangle is another often-created shape in both historical and modern-day mandalas. Although the triangle is not seen as frequently in nature as the circle, there are some examples of the shape; as seen in mountains, leaves, and crystals. Our beloved pets, all cats and some dogs, have perfectly formed triangular ears. The triangle can be manipulated to form a variety of angles and forms, unlike the circle which possesses a single design.

As with the circle, the triangle has been a deeply spiritual symbol in various religious traditions. In Christianity, the equilateral triangle represents the Holy Trinity (God as the Father, Son and Holy Spirit), and the triangle within a circle has been found in English churches symbolizing the eternity of the trinity (Pierce, 2014). In Hinduism, the triangle pointing upwards represents male energy, while the downward pointing triangle represents the female energy. Hinduism regards the triangle as preceding creation and representing nature (Khanna, 1979). The Greek capital letter *delta* is a triangle and symbolizes cosmic birth. In Buddhism, the Buddha is predominately pictured with legs crossed, forming a triangle, with the knees forming the base, and the head forming the tip of the triangle. The symbolism of the triangle represents the steady, grounded nature of the form. In Judaism, two interlocking equilateral triangles form the *Star of David*, the top triangle pointing to God, the bottom triangle pointing to the world.

In psychology, Carl Jung discussed the religious prominence of the triangle throughout time, and in various belief systems. Jung saw the trinity as an archetype of sorts, representing the triads of gods within one's prospective culture. In Jung's work, *A Psychological Approach to the Dogma of the Trinity* (1984), he states the following:

> *"Triads of gods appear very early, at the primitive level. The archaic triads in the religions of antiquity and of the East are too numerous to be mentioned here. Arrangement in triads is an archetype in the history of religion which in all probability formed the basis of the Christian Trinity."*
>
> -From *Psychology and Western Religion, 1984*

Jung himself experienced objection from some peers when attempting to explain the psychology behind the sacred idea of the trinity. He felt it was necessary, however, to examine such a symbol in religious traditions. He believed such a strong and meaningful symbol to many individuals would have to hold a deep and personal psychological truth within one's psyche (1984).

Jung believed that the trinity, represented by a triangle, seemed to be missing an important aspect of completion, a fourth element of sorts. He believed in the *quaternity*, an idea that the psyche moves towards completion in fours; fours comprising of two pairs of opposites. Jung felt the trinity was missing an important fourth element (the feminine for example), and often asked the question "Where's the fourth?" when speaking of the trinity symbol (1984).

Cultural anthropologist Angeles Arrien (1998) found the triangle to be a prominent shape in all cultures that she researched. She discovered that the triangle represented revelation and self-discovery within individuals. Triangles in artwork may symbolize focus, seeing one's goals, having a clear vision, and pursuing one's dreams in life.

The Square

The square is an integral part of many ancient mandalas and is often seen surrounding the mandala's circle. The square is a shape not seen in the natural world and is imagined to be a human creation. It is easy for us to name circular images in nature, and it's possible to think of triangular images as well. Trying to think of a natural creation in the shape of a square is an impossible task due to right angles solely being human creations.

Despite its non-existence in nature, the square has proven to be a valuable shape in most cultures and religions. In Hinduism, the square is seen as the receptacle or base of the world. It symbolizes the terrestrial world and the quality of orderliness (Khanna, 1979). In Tibetan Buddhism, the square represents firmness, stability and balance (Bryant, 1994). The square encases the circle in both Hindu and Buddhist yantras/mandalas, and contains the *four doors* previously described in Chapter 2. In Christianity, the square represents concepts of the number four, as in the four evangelists (Pierce, 2014). In early Christian art, the square was seen as a *nimbus* (more commonly known as a halo), behind the heads of saintly ones (Pierce, 2014). In Judaism, observant adult males wear a *tefillin,* two small black leather boxes worn on the left arm and forehead; the tefillin must be a perfect square. Inside the tefillin are scrolls containing words of the Torah. (Jewish Virtual Library, 2015). Although there are wide differences among the Native American tribes, the square was often seen as a symbol of the four cardinal directions and the four elements; it also symbolized stability, security and permanence (Dare to Discern, 2015).

Jung believed that the *squaring of the circle* was a natural progression towards the fulfillment of stability, and an archetype of wholeness (Jung,1992). Whereas the bindu (the center, most sacred part of the mandala) would represent the ego, the circle and bindu would represent the Self, and the square surrounding the circle would represent a deeper sense of Self, or full individuation. The square symbolized an orderly structure, a safe foundation of sorts, for the psyche to achieve wholeness. The idea of a *quaternity* represented wholeness (Jung, 1992).

In *Signs of Life: The Five Universal Shapes and How to Use Them* (1998), Angeles Arrien also recognizes the square as a symbol of stability. She states that drawing a square symbolizes a foundation, a deeper sense of security, upon which dreams and plans can be built. The square is a complete shape that shows integrity and accountability. Many cultures regarded the four points of the square as the foundations of life. Squares in artwork may signify the need for stability, order or balance.

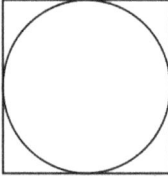

The Squaring of the Circle-Author created

Other Significant Shapes

The Equidistant Cross

The equidistant cross is probably more recognizable to Americans as the plus sign. Christians and non-Christians alike tend to think of the crucifix when imagining a cross, which has a longer piece designed to be representational of Jesus' body. However, the original cross symbol predates Christianity and was equidistant. It is believed that the equidistant cross may have been representative of kindling and symbolized the sacred fire

(Arrien, 1998). Possible symbolism among cultures shows the cross as a spiritual symbol of life, the union of heaven and earth, immortality, and, like the square, representing the four seasons and the four directions.

Angeles Arrien (1998) states that the equidistant cross represents relationships to ourselves and others. It shows the need to connect and integrate in an effort to become whole. It focuses on the quality of relationships, the time and effort spent with others, rather than on the quantity of the time spent. Crosses in artwork may suggest the need for relationships, integration and balance.

The Spiral

Spirals have been found throughout history in art, architecture and in nature. The triple spiral has been found in stone, most notably the Newgrange Monument in Ireland, dating back to approximately 3200 BCE. Single spirals were found in architecture during the Tang Dynasty of China. There is some debate as to the symbolism of the spiral, although the triple spiral in Christian art and architecture is believed to symbolize the Holy Trinity (Pierce, 2014).

Angeles Arrien (1998) explains that the spiral represents both growth and change. The spiral is a process, not a final product, in which we are evolving and changing. We are changing, and may return to common themes, but we are never quite where we started.

The spiral shows a need for variety, experiences, and changes in order to attain this evolution. Spirals in artwork may signify the need for flexibility, new options, or a new way of looking at things.

The Triple Spiral

The Heart

The heart is included in this book due to the multiple times I have personally noticed it in my clients' mandalas. Quite often, the heart is used as the bindu of their creations, or appearing in multiple places within the mandala. The symbol of the heart as seen above was not readily seen in art until approximately the 15th century. This depiction of the heart symbolizes love of all kinds, not just romantic love. When processing mandalas with my clients, those who have drawn hearts typically express positive feelings they are experiencing; feeling loved, valued and appreciated. I have often witnessed hearts with lines or an X through them, a jagged/separated heart, or a heart colored black instead of the traditional pink or red. When processing these hearts, clients typically verbalize their feelings of loss, sadness, and mistreatment by others.

The Star

When viewing the mandalas of my clients, stars also tend to be created often, both as a bindu, and throughout the mandala. Those who have studied symbology have noted the star typically symbolizes cosmic order, goddesses, pharaohs, or the soul. When processing my clients' mandalas, those who use stars typically express positive thoughts and feelings, as well as feeling smart, accomplished and improved. I personally wonder if the American school ideas of "Star Student" and getting a star sticker on student work help contribute to this idea.

Lines

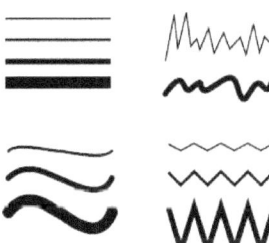

A large number of my clients use a variety of lines to help illustrate their personal mandalas. As a general theme, my clients have tended to stick with all straight, all jagged, or all curved lines within a mandala creation. It is rare for me to see a variety of lines used in their mandala artwork. This may simply be a matter of personal preference, or on a deeper level, their current emotional state. Art therapists have noted that scribbling is how all individuals begin the artistic process, and young children create spontaneous scribbles as a way to experiment (Malchiodi, 1999). These lines found in mandalas may be reaching back to these younger experiences, yet with a more definitive and purposeful style. Art therapists have noted that horizontal lines typically symbolize feelings of rest, vertical lines symbolize spirituality, diagonal lines connote movement, and curved lines represent energy (Malchiodi, 1999). When processing lines with my clients typically jagged lines are created when they are experiencing anxiety, anger or other states of distress, curved lines when they are experiencing calmness and tranquility.

Chapter 5

Color Use in Art and Psychotherapy

"Colors, like features, follow the changes of the emotions."
-Pablo Picasso

Few things can thrill us, repulse us, awaken us and cause distress in us as does color. One of the first questions often asked when getting to know someone is "What is your favorite color?" Color is a part of our most joyful celebrations, as well as our most debilitating events. From choosing pink or blue balloons to welcome a new edition, to picking bridesmaids' and flower colors for a wedding; from choosing paint colors for a new home to finalizing funeral colors after a loved one's death, color is absolutely a part of our lives. Despite the prominence of color in our lives, how often have we actually thought about color? What is color? Do we all see color the same? Is there a science to color, an art to color, a psychology to color? A short discussion on these questions can further enhance our personal use of color and further appreciate our clients' use of color.

The Science of Color

Color is not a tangible thing but rather is what our eyes see after light hits an object and is reflected and absorbed. To see color there must be light. The *visible spectrum* is a term used to describe the actual part of the electromagnetic spectrum that the human eye can actually see. This visible light corresponds to a wavelength range of 400 - 700 nanometers (nm) and a color range of violet through red (Morton, 2014). The color violet has the shortest wavelength which we can see; the color red has the longest wavelength. The order of colors from shortest to longest wavelength is: violet, blue, green, yellow, orange and red (Morton, 2014). This may cause one to ask: "Are black and white colors?" This may depend on who you ask! Black is formed by the complete absence of light (think when it is completely dark you cannot distinguish the colors of objects), so scientists do not consider it a color. Black is the absence of color. White, on the other hand, is all the wavelengths of the visible spectrum, or "all color", therefore white is scientifically considered a color. For purposes of this book, however, the focus will be on the six colors listed above, as black and white are referred to as "dark" and "light" when I work with children in a therapeutic setting.

Color originates from the light of the sun ("1" on illustration) whose rays are all colors, or white light. The white light then shines on an object ("2" on illustration), particular color rays are absorbed and reflected, and the resultant color is reflected by our eyes ("3" on illustration). The eyes send this message to the brain, and voila!, we instantly recognize an object by its color (Morton, 2014).

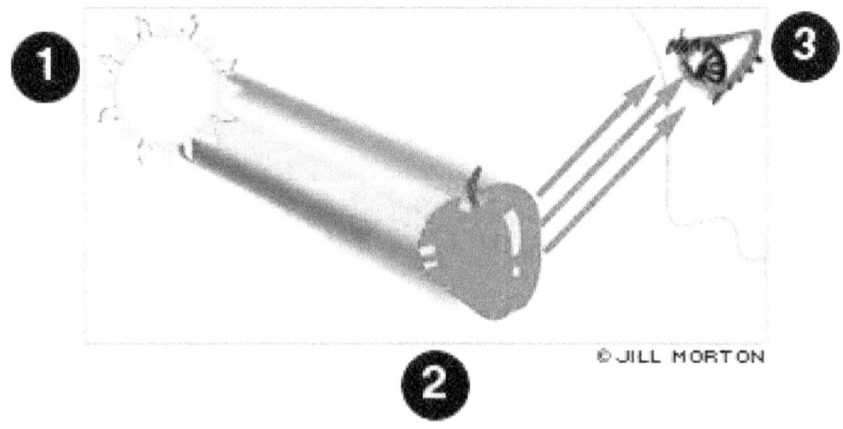

The Art of Color

The three properties to color are hue, intensity and value (Mollica, 2013). The *hue* of a color is the actual name of the color. The hue discerns one color from another, such as the color blue from the color red. The hue is dependent on its dominant wavelength, which gives it the unique color, yet it is independent of the particular lightness/darkness of the actual color. In color theory, the hue is considered a pure color, one free of any tint or shade (Mollica, 2013). The *intensity* of a color refers to the level of brightness of a color. The brightest intensity of a color would be the pure color/hue, the dullest intensity would be a color that is indiscernible and gray (Adding gray to a color is known as changing the tone of a color, thus affecting the intensity). The *value* of a color is the particular darkness or lightness of a color, created by adding white or black to the original hue. The term *shade* means adding black to a pure color; the term *tint* means adding white to a pure color (Mollica, 2013).

A *color wheel* is a term used to describe a visual tool showing the categories of colors and the relationships between them (Mollica, 2013). The primary colors on a color wheel are the hues red, yellow and blue; these colors are original and can be mixed to create many other colors. The secondary colors on a color wheel are the three colors created from the primary colors. The three secondary colors are orange (mix of yellow and red), green (mix of yellow and blue) and violet (mix of red and blue). The secondary colors can be thought of as the children of the primary colors. The tertiary colors on a color wheel are a result of mixing a primary color with its nearest secondary color on the color wheel. There are six tertiary colors: yellow-orange, red-orange, red-violet, blue-violet, blue-green and yellow-green. These twelve total colors are often known as the basic colors in which an endless variety of tints, shades and tones can be created (Mollica, 2013).

Artists have long used the theory of color harmony to create visually appealing works of art. Two particular examples are *complimentary* and *analogous* colors. Complimentary colors are those colors that are directly opposite each other on the color wheel, which create a vibrant, stand-out look. It is often used sparingly so as not to jar the observer. Analogous colors are those colors right next to each other on the color wheel; using these colors creates a calming, pleasing effect in artwork (Mollica, 2013).

It is interesting to note that the casual observer may have never realized the detail color plays in the art world, yet may still have felt the effects of the colors in play. Often in mandala creations clients will choose color combinations that follow the theory of color harmony without knowing of the theory in a cognitive sense.

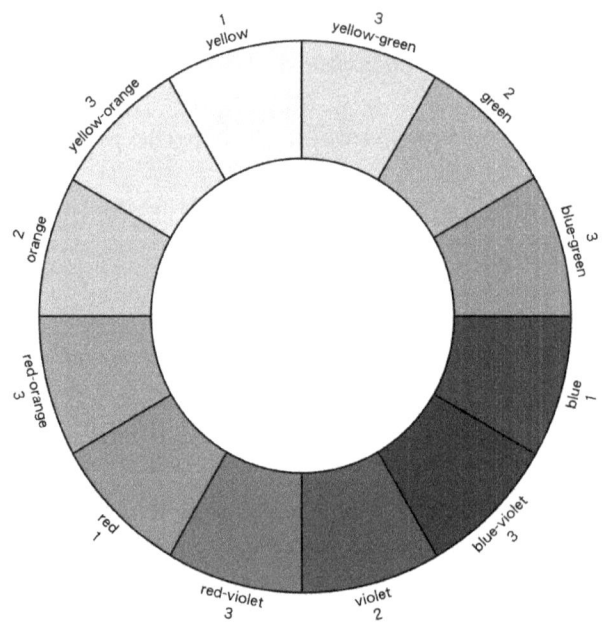

Color Wheel "1" showing primary, "2" secondary, "3" tertiary colors. www.sippdrawing.com

The Psychology of Color

For centuries, color has been studied and used to aid in the healing of individuals. The ancient Egyptians, Romans and Greeks are but a few examples of cultures that were known to use light for a variety of medical ailments. The Egyptians, in particular, are reported to have created *color rooms* to assist in healing. Using this color healing, an ill individual was evaluated , received a color diagnosis, and then put in an appropriate room with gems that would radiate the prescribed color into the room. Rubies and sapphires are two examples of gems that were used for this treatment (Art Therapy, 2005-2015).

Other ancient cultures have used colors to signify energy, from the Chinese who regarded color as energy *(chi)* circulating harmoniously throughout the body, to the Indian idea of *chakras*; seven energy centers in the body that help compliment a person's spiritual, mental, emotional and physical balance. Practices in color theory, or chromotherapy, continued throughout the Victorian Ages and the 1900's (Art Therapy, 2005-2015).

Modern day scientists tend to agree that color seems to create different emotional reactions for different individuals. Although the belief is that color is highly subjective depending on the viewer, a person's cultural, religious, and social background can indeed be factors into a preference of colors (O'Connor, 2011). Many other popular beliefs of color, such as the wavelengths of color affecting emotions, and certain colors producing calming affects, have largely not been proven due to a lack of statistical significance. Scientists caution against wholeheartedly believing that a color has certain intrinsic qualities, but rather that age, culture, society, and gender can be more accurate in determining color preference (O'Connor, 2011).

Therapists working with children are encouraged to complete a color assessment with clients prior to introducing art interventions to more fully understand each particular client's preferences. There are many art and play therapy interventions that have been created to match clients' emotions to colors, which can provide great insight into future artwork created by the client. A simple assessment is having clients fill in a *My Emotional Circles* sheet (see page 40) with whichever color they deem appropriate. Four circles have a feeling word written in the center, while two circles are blank for the client to list two additional feelings. The final product can be saved to use as a tool when assessing future client artwork. Individual assessment by far is the superior method to discovering the emotional language created by color within clients.

While realizing the importance of individual preference into the psychology of color, it may be helpful for therapists to have a general knowledge of some common color associations found in particular cultures. Below is a brief description of the six main colors, and some broad associations with each of them. This information is based upon the book *If It's Purple, Someone's Gonna Die: The Power of Color in Visual Storytelling* (Bellantoni, 2014); a reference commonly used in American film and cinematography university courses to further understand the power of color.

Red: Often feels to the viewer as angry, powerful, defiant, lusty and/or anxious
Yellow: Often feels to the viewer as exuberant, obsessive, daring and/or cautionary
Blue: Often feels to the viewer as cerebral, passive, melancholy and/or cold
Orange: Often feels to the viewer as warm, naive, exotic and/or toxic
Purple: Often feels to the viewer as illusory, fantastic, mystical and/or asexual
Green: Often feels to the viewer as healthy, vital, ambivalent, and/or ominous

There have also been cultural associations to particular colors as noted by cultural anthropologists and art therapists. Some of the common associations are listed below.

Red: Good luck in China and India, revolution in Russia, halting in the U.S., celebratory in Spain, seen on buses and phone booths in the U.K.

Yellow: Happiness and prosperity in Egypt, caution in the U.S., imperial color in China

Blue: Holiness in Judaism and Islam, sadness in the U.S., mercy in India

Orange: Renunciation in Hinduism and some Buddhism sects, love in China and Japan, Halloween and construction in the U.S.

Purple: Wealth and royalty in most ancient cultures, penitence in Christianity, bravery in the U.S. (Purple Heart)

Green: Nature in most cultures, envy and sickness in the U.S.

(Art Therapy Blog, 2005-2015)

It is an excellent resource for therapists to have an idea of how color is used in our society and other cultures. We often feel a particular way about a color without realizing our influences from television, film, artwork, and nature. This societal influence can help us begin to process the artwork of our clients, while also remembering the great importance of individual tastes and preferences. The exceptional therapist will have knowledge of color in our society and world, while also fully processing each client's emotions towards colors.

My Emotional Circles
©Tracy Turner-Bumberry

Created by_____ on_____

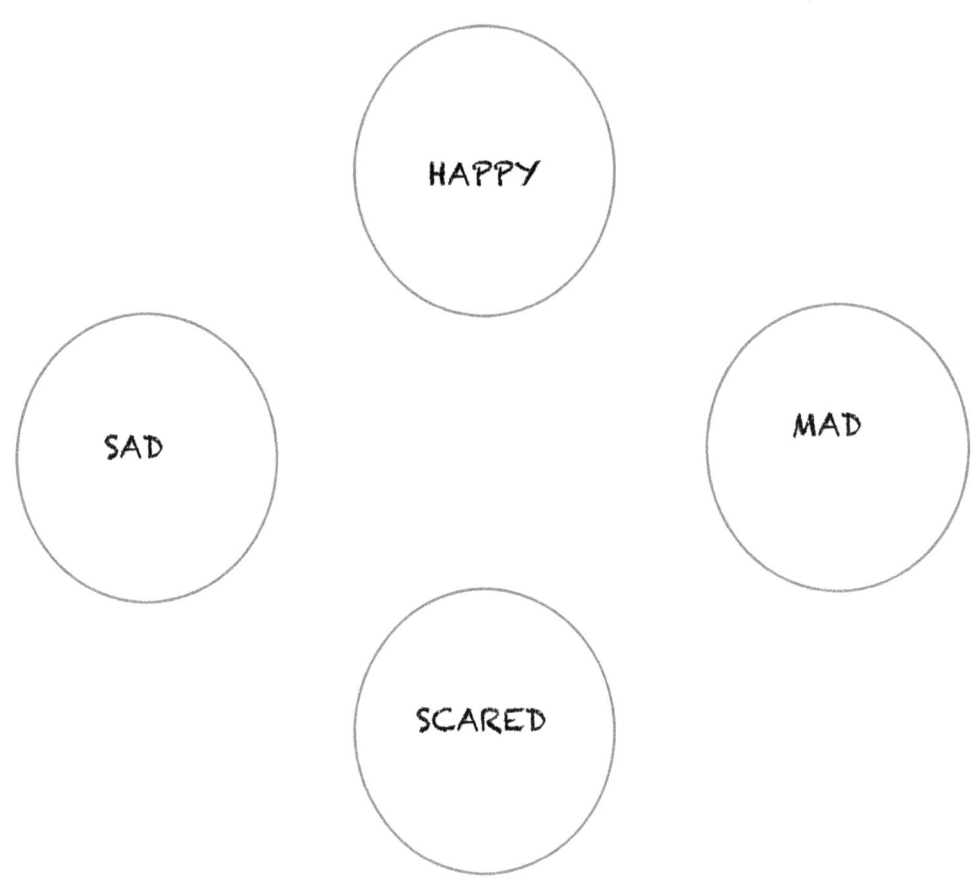

Chapter 6

Current Research on Using Mandalas in Psychotherapy

"Research is to see what everybody else has seen, and to think what nobody else has thought."
-Albert Szent-Gyorgyi

In 2014 I attended a play therapy workshop on various interventions to employ with children in crisis. This presenter, in speaking of the therapist's duty to choose meaningful interventions, made the following statement which has stayed with me when planning each play therapy session. He stated that although therapists hold different ideas on the counseling theories they utilize, and may perform a variety of directive interventions, the real test is whether the intervention chosen is appropriate and helpful to the client. A therapist should ask when planning each client intervention, "Why am I choosing this intervention? How can this intervention best help my client? Could I explain to anyone, from a parent to a supervisor why this intervention was the one chosen?"

It is not merely important but vital to ensure that the right intervention is created for each client a therapist sees. If we are simply choosing art or play interventions at random, or for reasons not pertinent to the client issue, we are not fulfilling our vital role as change agents for the client. Child therapists hold an important duty to ensure that appropriate treatment is given to our clients due to the fact that our clients may be initially unaware of what is truly needed to heal and grow. An adult client may have the insight and reasoning skills to determine when a therapist is helping versus when the sessions may not be beneficial to them. A child client, especially one working with an art or play therapist, may be having such a fun time creating works of art prescribed by the therapist that, although some growth may occur from creating such art, true therapeutic treatment may not be occurring. It is our duty as child therapists to ensure that our clients are getting the best care possible, and the most effective art and play therapy interventions for them.

One way to ensure this is occurring is by taking a thorough initial evaluation to discover current strengths and difficulties within the client. Knowing all clients' true developmental level, as opposed to chronological age, helps the therapist create appropriate interventions. It is futile to attempt interventions that are beyond the clients current level of understanding and development. Maintaining detailed progress notes; processing the affect noted during the interventions, important verbal and non-verbal statements, and any potential take-away the client had from completing the intervention is essential as well. Consistently reviewing the child's treatment plan, and assessing the growth made towards individual treatment goals is a third important step. Yet another way of predicting an intervention's success lies in any previous research done on this intervention.

Limited research is a weakness in many art and play therapy interventions. Within the past few years there have been further advances in art and play therapy research, yet more information is needed to be on par with other areas of counseling research. It is important for therapists to be aware of any research conducted in the areas of art and play therapy interventions, to further ensure that the interventions chosen can be of benefit to their clients. Having the ability to cite research that shows the effectiveness of an intervention completed in a therapeutic setting helps answer the question, "Why did I choose this intervention for this client?"

This chapter will highlight a few research studies conducted on the effectiveness of creating mandalas with a variety of childhood disorders. Highlighted are research studies that reveal statistically significant benefit upon completion of a mandala intervention. This will hopefully lead child therapists toward the desire to research art and play interventions more often, in a thoughtful and engaging manner.

Drawing Within the Circle

While creating his own mandalas, Carl Jung discovered the importance of drawing within a circle. In *Mandala Symbolism* (1992), he discussed this realization of his own inner situations being drawn within the circle; cryptograms of his true self. He viewed the circle as a form of protection in which the deeper workings of the self could be discovered. When creating within the circle, Jung found a healing of sorts, which then prompted him to use mandala interventions with his clients. He also noticed a sense of calm and relaxation with his clients who created these drawings in his care.

Many modern day art therapists agree with the belief that drawing within a circle creates relaxation and relief within clients. Joan Kellogg has attributed creating within a circle to be somewhat of a hypnotic experience (1978).

There was an interesting study conducted by Maralynn Slegelis (1987) to test Jung's idea on the relaxing effects of drawing within the circle. Thirty-two college students created artwork within a circle and a square. She specifically looked for the differences in the number of angles drawn within the circle versus the square (holding the psychological assumption that angles represent frustration whereas curvilinear markings show relaxation). Her hypothesis that fewer angles would be created within the circle was proven to be correct with statistical significance noted.

Post Traumatic Stress Disorder

A study was conducted on the effects of mandala creations to participants' reduction of PTSD symptoms. The results of this study were detailed in the research article entitled *Empirical Study on the Healing Nature of Mandalas,* in the 2007 edition of the journal *Psychology of Aesthetics, Creativity, and the Arts.* (Please see the References section for more information on this study). The study consisted of 36 undergraduate students, 17 in the control group, 19 in the experimental group. Each participant was pre-screened for traits of PTSD using appropriate treatment screenings, and those exhibiting moderate levels of PTSD symptoms were chosen. The participants would all be involved in drawing sessions over three consecutive days.

Both groups were given crayons, paper and a pencil to complete their tasks. They were all given twenty minutes to complete each daily activity. The control group was instructed to draw a particular item on each of the three days. The experimental group was asked to draw a large circle on the paper, and then fill in the circle with shapes and symbols relating to their trauma. The results of the study showed that those in the experimental group had a significant reduction of PTSD symptoms immediately after, and at a one month follow up visit.

Attention Deficit Hyperactivity Disorder

Several single case studies have been completed showing the effectiveness of mandala creations with ADHD clients. One study conducted by Smitherman, Brown and Church (1996) specifically tested the effects mandala creations had on children with ADHD. The mandala was used as an active centering tool for clients in art therapy who had the diagnosis of ADHD. During specified intervals of treatment, the therapist would request a drawing to be completed. By using a formal examination scale, the researchers concluded that creating mandalas helped reduce impulsivity while increasing attention in those clients.

Anxiety

Nancy Curry and and Tim Kasser were interested in studying the effect of particular art therapy interventions in treating anxiety (2005). Their experiment was conducted on eighty-four undergraduate students, who first responded as to their current levels of anxiety. They were next given an anxiety induction, in which they had to recall an anxiety provoking situation, and then spend four minutes writing about this experience. After this, an anxiety inventory was again completed. The participants were then randomly assigned to one of three tasks; coloring a mandala, coloring a plaid form, or coloring on a blank sheet of paper. Each coloring group was kept together in a space so as not to have individuals looking to see what others were coloring. The participants were asked to color for twenty minutes, then a final anxiety assessment was completed.

Those that colored in mandalas were found to have statistically significant lower anxiety scores as compared to those who free-form colored for twenty minutes. It was also found that those who colored the plaid form had lowered anxiety as well. It was additionally found that those who colored in the mandala had anxiety rates even lower than their original assessments given before the anxiety induction.

Future Findings

Positive therapeutic effects of coloring and creating mandalas have been shown through other research studies in addition to those highlighted in this book. The issue remains that much of this research has small sample sizes and are completed on a relatively rare basis. Many art and play therapists have discovered the great benefits of mandala creation as a viable, therapeutic intervention with their clients. Perhaps those of us in the therapy profession should consider creating opportunities for additional research to be completed.

Chapter 7

Guidelines for Mandala Use in Psychotherapy

"Think of your head as an unsafe neighborhood; don't go there alone."
-Augusten Burroughs

Child therapists are continually seeking meaningful interventions that will both engage and heal their clients. When conducting workshops, I am often asked for specific interventions that can be used for a variety of ages, levels and/or abilities. Mandala interventions are special in that they can be used universally in a therapeutic setting. From coloring a pre-made mandala, to completing a strictly non-directive one, mandala interventions are a reliable tool to be used in the session.

At this point, therapists may see the value of using mandalas in the playroom but may have questions regarding the steps in using them. Although therapists' styles may differ, it is important to provide a similar setting, explanation, and process so the client can achieve the full level of healing and relaxation that creating mandalas can provide. This chapter will highlight how to prepare a therapy room for mandala creation, how to introduce the particular intervention to the client, guidelines while the client is creating, and a technique for processing the mandala. These detailed steps are necessary to fully enhance the therapeutic experience for mandala creation.

When to Use the Mandala

Before any explanation on preparing a therapy room for mandala interventions, one may be asking when is the ideal time to use the mandala in the course of client treatment. Professional judgement is to be used to determine this. It is important that a client feels comfortable and trusts the therapist before creating any type of directive or non-directive piece of art. Mandala work is deeply personal and can be too revealing for clients if they are not feeling a relationship yet with the therapist. Initially while building rapport however, the therapist could certainly use pre-made mandalas the client could color during the session. This intervention can help relax the client, and build the free and protected space which is so important in any therapy room. As the relationship builds, more creative mandala interventions can be used which will greatly enhance the therapeutic process.

Setting up the Mandala Session

As with any client entering the therapy room, the room should be clean, bright, uncluttered and feel open and engaging. The mandala circle should already be cut if using paper, or out and visible if using paper plates, foam, wood, etc. In my professional experience I have had few children who enjoy creating artwork at a table, so I have a very comfy spot on the floor, with a soft rug and fluffy pillows. The prepared mandala medium for the session would either be clipped on a clipboard or placed on a tray table. Any additional supplies would be in close proximity to the client. Although care is taken to have a multitude of supplies on hand and nearby, I make it clear during the introduction that if another item is needed but not visible, to please let me know so I can retrieve it. I also have a large singing bowl with a striker I use to begin the mandala sessions. Clients are welcome to use this bowl and striker to indicate completion of their artwork. Finally, I have a music source close at hand in the event that clients feel any anxiety by my silence or create better with music.

Introducing the Mandala Intervention

As clients enter the session, I enjoy hearing about their day and any joys or sorrows that they may have experienced since we last met. I would never want to skip this part of the session in order to introduce a mandala intervention. However, as most art and play therapists know, play is a child's natural language, so it typically does not take long for the client to soon exclaim "What are we going to do today?" Introducing the mandala intervention for the first time may be as important as the processing phase, secondary only to the clients' creation of the mandala. Although I provide a possible script to use in Chapter 8, I leave it to the therapists' judgement to use those words and phrases that they best feel describes the mandala artwork process. I will highlight several key points below to consider when planning the introduction:

- Explain the meaning of the word mandala (magic circle).
- Briefly discuss how mandalas have been used throughout the centuries to promote relaxation and healing.
- Describe how most mandalas have the center as the most sacred part of the mandala (bindu).
- Invite the clients to fill in the circle with any shapes, symbols, colors, scribbles, pictures, or words that they wish for a non-directive mandala. For a directive mandala explain the procedure to complete the particular mandala.
- Remind the clients, whether it is a directive or a non-directive mandala that there is no wrong way to create it; they should focus on what they believe is the right way to create.

- Explain that you will be quiet during their creation phase so they can better focus on their artwork.
- Make sure to remind the clients to tell you when they are finished; too often therapists say "Are you done?" which can lead the clients to feel pressure to be finished, even if they are not.
- Have a word or sound that begins the creation phase and ends the creation phase. Bells, gongs or mantras are wonderful transitional tools.

Creation Phase

The creation phase is the active process of the client making the mandala. The client has received the instruction, the materials are within reach, and the magic can begin. This is a very important time for the therapist as well, for this is the time where silence is needed. I refer to this as *active silence*; the moments where I am consciously and deliberately remaining silent, while also remaining aware and close to the client.

The idea, as well as the act of silence can be very difficult for many therapists. Often times, therapists may feel uncomfortable actively being silent, while clients may feel awkward creating during silence. This may largely be based on our westernized culture, where pauses in conversation and silence as a whole are largely ignored. Several studies have shown that Western culture tends to rely on less pauses in conversations than Eastern cultures (Ting-Toomey, 1999). One particular study (Endrass et. al. 2008) compared the amount of one and two second pauses with Germans in conversation versus the amount of the same-timed pauses with Japanese individuals. The results showed that in a typical, five minute conversation the German participants on average had 7, one-second pauses, and 1, two or more second pauses. In comparison, the Japanese subjects had 31, one-second pauses, and 8, two or more second pauses. On the whole, European cultures have often been denoted as being verbose, controlling with speech, and rude, due to the lack of silence and pauses in conversation (Ting-Toomery, 1999). This helps explain why the idea of silence may feel foreign to us, and our clients. However, it is during these active silence moments where clients can freely create, without feeling the need to stop, explain, or have idle chit-chat with the therapist. It is the duty of the therapist to continue practicing active silence, where no words are spoken, but an alert, welcoming presence is felt by the client. With practice, silence becomes less awkward and more enjoyable to the therapist and the client. If some clients are having a particularly difficult time creating due to the silence, music may be used to help the client feel more comfortable. Gently discussing client discomfort could also be a beneficial tool during the processing phase.

Processing the Mandala

Processing clients' mandalas can be a revealing and enlightening treat for the therapist. Clients are able to discuss the art they created and further think about the meaning of their artwork. Those therapists who have already been using art and play interventions in the therapy room have seen the great value processing artwork can hold. It is important to note that many clients do not wish to process their artwork for a variety of reasons. Therapists should not automatically assume that this is due to client resistance or to a healthy rapport not being met. Some clients feel a great sense of relief while creating their artwork and do not see a need to verbalize their creations. As a rule of thumb, I tend to ask the client each time a piece of art is created if they would like to process it, regardless of how many no responses I may have previously received. It is important not to assume that clients don't want to share any of their artwork, rather that some pieces they create may not wish to be shared. Processing can also occur during later sessions if the therapist feels that the particular mandala created may need some verbal explanation, while still respecting the healing that can occur simply through creating.

Each therapist has his or her unique and personal style that must be authentic when processing any art intervention, and mandalas are no exception. Therapists can only be effective when they are genuine. Because of this, I am hesitant to give a full script of how to process a mandala intervention. A script can feel unnatural to the therapist and rehearsed to the clients. Although I do give a brief script in Chapter 8 of this book, I also want to give a list of questions that has shown to be thought provoking and insightful during processing. All, some, or a few of the questions can be asked, based on the particular mandala created. Therapists should remember to keep the processing time conversational and natural; allowing the client to determine what and how much to express, while the therapist helps guide the processing with questions.

Many mandala interventions provided in this book warrant additional questions which may further highlight the creation. Chapter 8 contains each mandala intervention, and any additional questions can be found towards the bottom of the mandala explanation, in the *Discussion* section.

Questions When Processing a Mandala Intervention

© Tracy Turner-Bumberry

- All artists give their masterpieces titles, even if it's simply "Untitled". What name would you give your masterpiece? (I used to get many "I don't know" responses when I simply asked what the title of their art would be. Since adding these extra words I almost always get a response.)

- Let's talk about this work of art. What's happening in this masterpiece?

- I've noticed (point out a particular area, color, shape). Please tell me more.

- What feelings did you feel before creating this work of art? While creating this work of art? Now?

- I noticed that you _____ while creating this part. What do you think about this? (Examples include scrunched eyes, hard pressure of writing instrument, tears, sighing, etc.)

- Looking at your masterpiece now, do you wonder about any parts of it? (I often explain how after creating, we may look at our art and say, "I wonder why I did _____?")

- Let's pretend we could jump into your mandala. Let's do it now. (I dramatize this by counting to 3 and then mimic diving in) How does it feel to be in your mandala? What do we notice now that we are in the mandala? (I help facilitate this by talking about the senses, what do we now see, hear, feel, smell, taste.)

- Your therapy goal has been _____. How do you think creating this masterpiece may have gotten you closer to this goal? (I personally love tying in interventions to the goal!)

- What did you learn from creating this work of art? (This can be anything, about themselves, their abilities, their strengths, their fears, etc.)

Always make sure to take a picture of the mandala, and give the client the option of keeping the mandala in the file or taking it home.

Chapter 8

Mandala Interventions to Use With Children

"All art requires courage"
-Anne Tucker

Mandala interventions are for all ages and skill levels. The interventions highlighted in this book are identified for use with children, but therapists will recognize that teens, adults, couples, seniors and groups could benefit from these interventions as well. Certain materials are necessary for any mandala intervention. The child therapist will likely have these materials, but for other therapist professionals you will need:

- Scissors
- Compass (Many therapists have pre-drawn circles, yet some clients like to create their own mandala size. Circle stencil templates can also be bought at office supply stores and are easier for children to use.)
- Crayons
- Pastels
- Colored pencils
- Markers
- Pencils
- Erasers
- Glue (many mandalas are glued onto another surface or items are glued onto the mandala)
- Multi-media materials such as gems, stickers, stamps, glitter, etc.
- Most importantly, templates for mandalas (I use white and colored paper, paper plates, foam and wood circles)

There are two types of mandalas to create, directive or non-directive. Non-directive mandalas are for the clients who enjoy the act of creating, using vivid imagination, and having the freedom to start from no concept to completion. These clients may love to be in control and enjoy challenge and mastery. They may also feel more comfortable and have gained sufficient rapport with the therapist. Non-directive mandalas can be initiated by the therapist using a similar dialogue to the following script:

"Today we will create a piece of art known as a mandala. This is an ancient word that means circle. The most magical part of a mandala is the center (bindu), where artists typically begin by designing a special object or symbol in the center. Then, the artist creates outward in whatever way he/she feels drawn to do. Please use this circle to create your mandala and begin when you feel ready. Feel free to fill up this circle with whatever shapes, pictures, colors, words, or anything that you wish. Make it your own. I will ring the gong to start the process, and I will remain quiet so you can create. Let me know when you are finished, and we can talk about your art if you wish. Please remember to tell me when you are done, or ring the gong so I know. If you need anything, please let me know."

Using the above wording, or something similar, is giving clients the basic understanding of the mandala without affecting their own creativity. I discourage showing pictures or images of mandalas, since this not only affects their creativity, but may have them focus on the evenness and detail of traditional mandalas rather than their own creative energies.

As with all mandala creations, it is beneficial for the therapist to mentally process during the creation and verbally process after with the client to measure if deeper levels of relaxation have occurred during the act of mandala creation.

Directive mandalas are helpful for those clients who are experiencing a specific issue to process, are anxious about creating artwork, have very concrete thinking skills, or who may need a gentle push to get their creative juices flowing. Often these mandalas feel less threatening to the client who has not yet established a firm rapport with the therapist.

These interventions often use a variety of materials, are decided beforehand by the therapist, and clearly communicate the direction of the mandala artwork. A directive mandala intervention should be carefully and thoughtfully chosen by the therapist, and the rationale for the intervention should be explainable at any time. It may not be beneficial for the client to randomly complete a hodgepodge of art activities in a therapy session; directive art activities are wonderful tools when chosen specifically to meet a client's needs.

The following pages detail fifty mandala interventions for therapist use. Each page details the title of the mandala intervention, the materials needed, the suggested population and use, and instructions. Please note that all of these activities can be tailored and redesigned to best help each particular client. Modifications often provide more powerful artwork and a more successful session. Although an age range and suggested use is given, please note that liberty can be taken with this as well. Therapists are key to knowing their individual clients and what each needs to facilitate growth.

Introducing directive mandalas is similar to the script for non-directive mandalas, with the exception that specific instructions are given to the client. Therapists should check for understanding from the client, and fully allow any modification or idea that the client has. Processing, based on Chapter 7, is essential with these mandalas as well.

There are some general instructions for opening the process of creating a mandala. **This is step #1 for all mandala interventions to give clients some insight into mandalas.** Step #1 begins by briefly explaining the history of creating mandalas to help people relax and better understand themselves. Explain how some mandalas are created with music as inspiration, and that soft music can help creativity blossom. Discuss how the center of the mandala (bindu) is where an artist begins the mandala creation, and then moves outward. Let the clients know that there is no right or wrong way to create a mandala, and it is best to just start creating without thinking too hard about what they wish to create. Let them know that you will remain quiet during their creation, and to please let you know when they are finished. They can also indicate completion by ringing the gong. At this point, give the specific directions for the particular mandala, ask if there are any questions, and then tell them to begin. Ring the gong.

One final note, I create these mandalas myself before giving the interventions to clients. This allows me to experience the power and healing nature of the mandala, discover alternative ways to present the activity, and give myself the needed self-care essential for our profession. As most of us know, but often forget, compassion towards ourselves is vital to fully have compassion for others. Mandala creation is one beautiful way to allow gentle compassion within ourselves.

ALL FULL COLOR MANDALAS CAN BE SEEN AT WWW.KSCOUNSELINGSTL.COM

Mandala #1

Name: Non-directive Mandala

Level: All ages as well as groups

Materials: Circle template, pencil, eraser, ruler

Procedure:
Follow Step #1 (page 56)

Discussion:
The gong is a useful tool to signal the beginning and ending of the creation without having to use words. The sound of the gong reverberates for an extended period of time, and often helps with the free-flow of ideas. A candle may also be lit to better prepare the sacred space of the therapy room.

Often times, clients may feel internal pressure to create a specific work of art, and/or may feel that they need more instruction from the therapist. Although the therapist may feel uncomfortable and wish to give more guidance, it is important to trust the process, and accept that the client has the ability to overcome this need for direction. If the client uses words such as "I can't do this!" or "This is hard!", gently remind him/her that anything created is special since it is his/her work of art.

When the client has expressed completion, allow for processing by asking the questions detailed in Chapter 7.

Non-Directive Mandala

(Created by a 12 year old client who chose to take it home, color, and return. Titled "Floral Art".)

Non-Directive Mandala

(Titled: "Peace", created by 7 year old client)

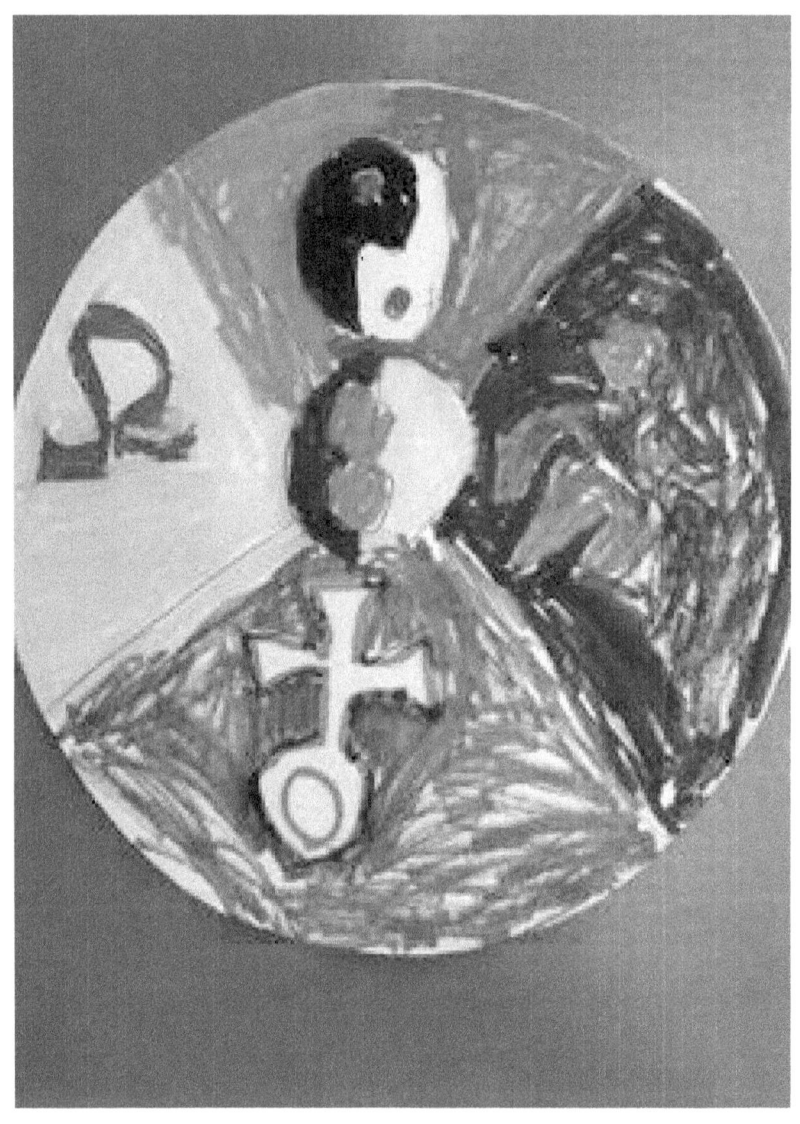

Non Directive Mandala

(Titled "Earth", created by 7 year old client using paint, glue and glitter)

Non-Directive Mandala

(Titled "Love", created by 4 year old client using a paper plate as a mandala template)

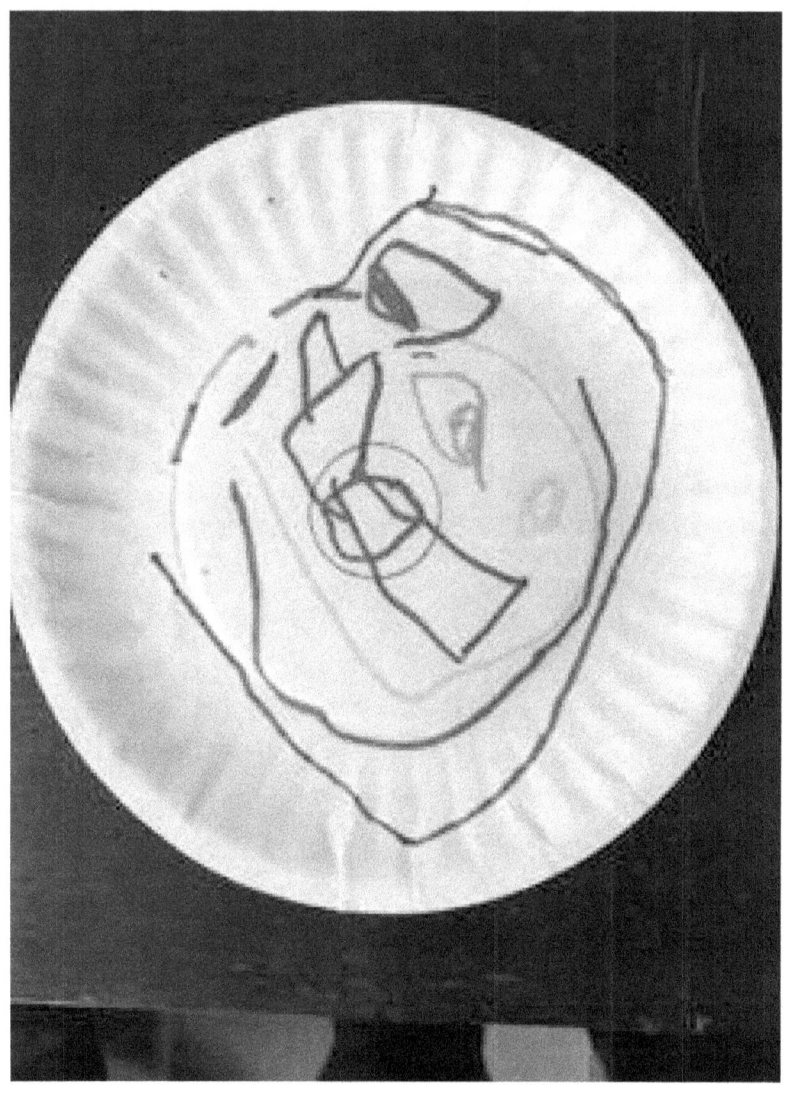

Non-Directive Mandala

(Created by 16 year old client, untitled)

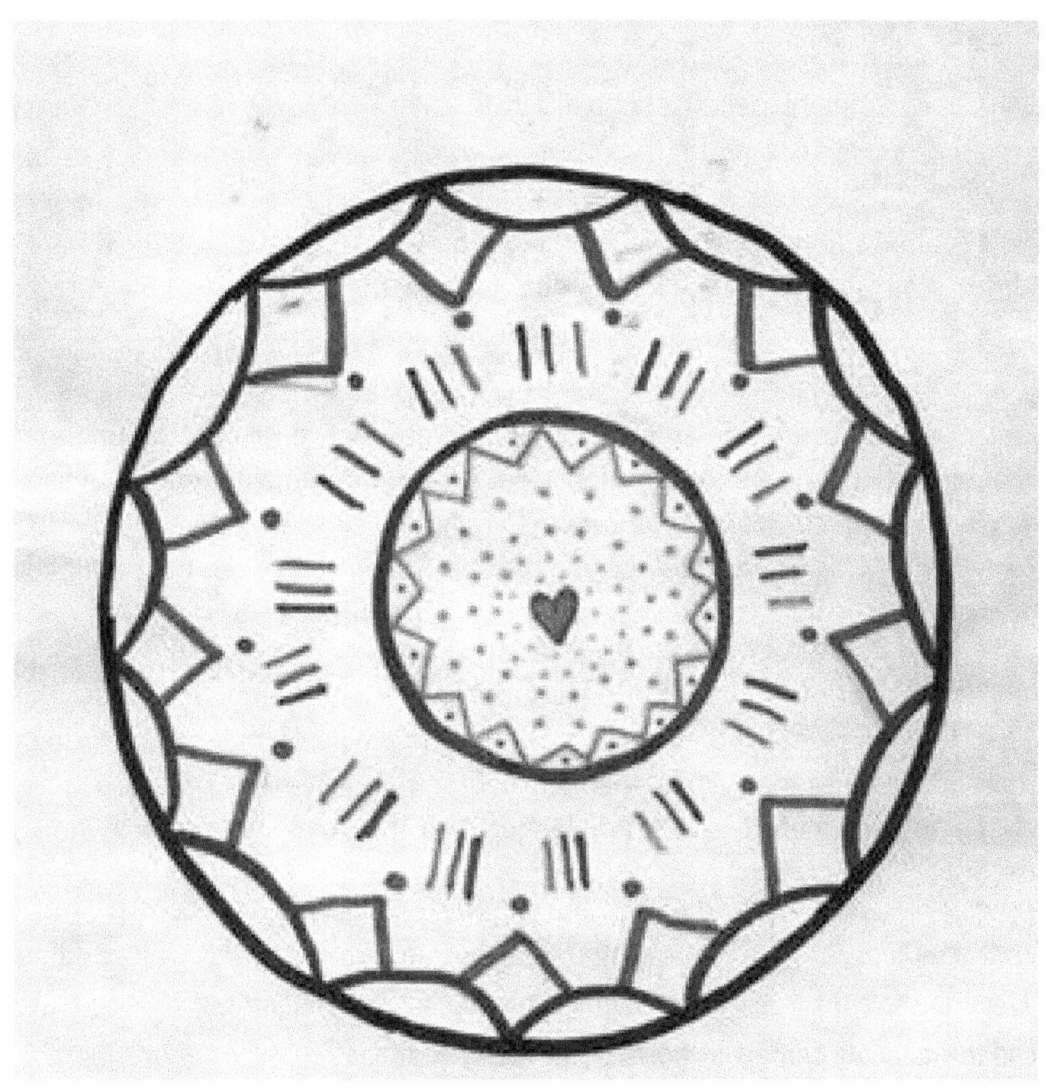

Mandala #2

Name: Music Mandala

Level: All ages

Materials: Circle template, pencil, classical music, ruler

Procedure:
After Step #1, allow clients to choose a particular classical CD or station in which to aid with their creations. Tell them they may begin, and ring the gong.

Discussion:
Notice this mandala is very similar to the original non-directive mandala, with the addition of background music. Many clients feel uncomfortable with total silence, so the music may help them feel more comfortable. Other clients feel more creative and emotionally open when listening to classical music, fostering depth in their mandala creation.

A modification is to allow clients to bring in music of their choosing. Sometimes these musical genres are new to the therapist. By allowing any type of music to be brought into the session, the therapist may gain valuable insight into the clients' world. The benefits outweigh the potential negatives of crude language or loud melodies that may be otherwise disturbing.

As with all mandalas, use the processing questions found in Chapter 7 while adding:
- Describe how the music inspired you either positively or negatively.
- Did the mandala change as parts of the music changed?
- What are the similarities/differences between the mandala created and the music?

Mandala #3

Name: Sand Mandala

Level: All ages

Materials: Sand tray with sand, collection of miniatures

Procedure:
Detail Step #1. Next explain to the client that today's mandala will be created in the sand. The client will create the circle using his/her finger in the sand to make a circle depression. Explain that all of the miniatures in the therapy room may be used within the circle to make this mandala. Guide the client to first choose an item for the center, and then create outwards. Remind the client that there is no "right" or "wrong" way to create a mandala, and it is best to just start creating without thinking too hard about what he/she wants to create. Remind the client about your silence during the creation, and to please indicate when finished by telling you or by ringing the gong. Begin by ringing the gong.

Discussion:
Sand brings an additional sensory element to the mandala creation process. Many therapists readily have a sand tray and miniatures at their disposal. However, modifications can be made for therapists who do not have these materials. Rice, lentils, water beads, uncooked beans, and beads have all been used in a tub to substitute for sand. If these are used, place a circle template on the materials for a proper visual. Substitutions for miniatures include stickers, stones, leaves, and general knick knacks in the therapy room.

Discussion questions remain the same with the following additions:
- **Explain the feelings involved with using the sand.**
- **Were there any miniatures you wanted to use that I did not have? What were they? How did you compensate?**

Sand Mandala

(Created by 8 year old client using a large stone heart as center, rocks as first layer, and glass beads of various colors. Titled "An Open Heart")

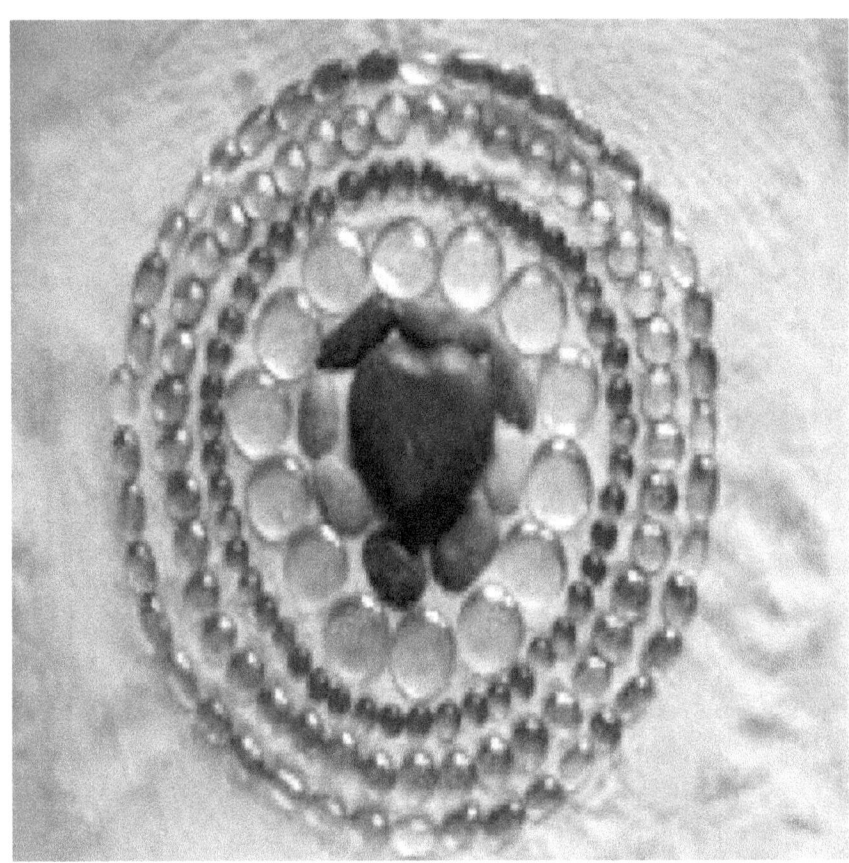

Mandala #4

Name: Nature Mandala

Level: All ages and can be done in groups

Materials: Paper bag, white sheet, pieces of nature (found during a nature walk is ideal)

Procedure:
Explain that you both will be going on a nature walk to collect pieces of nature. Make sure the client understands the importance of respecting nature, and only picking up those items that are no longer growing (For example, a child picking a rose off of a neighbor's bush is not respecting nature.) Tell client to pick up any items that catches his/her eye. Provide client with a paper bag in which items can be collected. If the therapist does not have the ability to take a client outside, or does not have pieces of nature in the outside environment, the counselor may bring nature into the therapy room. After the walk, follow Step #1. Detail how sand mandalas take weeks to create and then are allowed to blow away to show how nothing is permanent. Explain that this is known as impermanence. The nature items will be used to construct a mandala which will then be destructed as well. Provide a folded white sheet, and have the client begin creating the mandala, focusing first on the center and then moving outwards. Remind the client about your silence and to indicate the completion of the mandala, either verbally or by ringing the gong. Begin by ringing the gong.

Discussion:
This intervention has proven to be a favorite with my clients. Nature items seem to hold a significant place within people, and the multi-textured items seem to help with regulation and peace. Less emphasis is placed on fine motor skill (such as is needed for drawing), so there is very little resistance towards beginning. Group members can also create nature mandalas, each contributing from their own nature bags. The dismantling part of the mandala has proven difficult with some clients. Carrying the sheet together outside, and then letting "nature take its course" seems to be the best way to symbolize the idea of impermanence. If the client appears too troubled by this, it would be best for the therapists to allow the mandala to remain until after the client leaves the session. Remind the client that a photo will be taken, and that he/she may have a copy at the next session.

Discussion questions remain the same with the following additions:

- Describe the feelings with walking first and then creating your mandala.
- Describe the feeling of placing your mandala back into nature.

Nature Mandala

(Created by a six year old client titled "Autumn". He especially seemed drawn to leaves, and used two leaves for the bindu since he couldn't decide. This client had no issue with dismantling his mandala.)

Mandala #5

Name: Thumbprint Mandala

Level: All ages and groups

Materials: Mandala template, a variety of washable ink stamp pads in various colors, wet paper towels or baby wipes to clean clients' thumbs between color changes

Procedure:
Follow Step #1. Hand the client the mandala template and explain that today's mandala will be created by only using colored stamp pads and their thumbs. Invite them to use whatever colors they wish to create a masterpiece on the circle. Remind client to wash off the thumb when changing colors to keep the colors clear. The client can use as many or few colors as desired to create this masterpiece. Begin by ringing the gong.

Discussion:
This mandala creation involves an extra sensory component of touch which can be very therapeutic for many clients. Whereas getting an entire hand messy can be overwhelming for some clients, the lone thumb seems to be a safe boundary and feasible for most, if not all clients. Although it is always advisable to remain quiet during mandala creations, therapists may need to help clients remember to wipe off their thumbs when changing colors. I have forgotten to do this, and have often had clients upset that their colors were mixed! If this does occur the therapist can allow the client to start over, or give a reminder that there really are no mistakes in works of art and encourage him/her to continue.

Discussion questions remain the same with the following addition:
- How did it feel to use your thumb to create your masterpiece?
- How could you use your thumb/fingers/hands in other artistic ways to help you relax?

Mandala #6

Name: Floral mandala

Level: All ages and suitable for groups

Materials: Sand tray/large white paper/sheet, bouquet of flowers (variety of colors and sizes and include greenery), scissors

Procedure:
Follow Step #1. Discuss how mandalas have been created with sand, paper, rocks, metals, etc., and explain how the flowers will be used to create the mandala. Describe that any or all parts of a flower may be used, and that the flowers can be cut, torn or manipulated in whatever way the client chooses. Have the client begin creating the mandala on the provided base. Remind the client to focus first on the center and then move outwards. Remind him/her that you will be remaining quiet during the creation, and to please let you know when finished. He/she can also indicate completion by ringing the gong. Begin by ringing the gong.

Discussion:
This type of mandala has proven very popular with clients. Planning needs to occur ahead of time to ensure flowers are available, although some therapists keep a ready supply of fresh flowers in vases in case the client chooses this intervention. A possible modification is to use silk flowers, but it may be a poor substitute for the sensory stimulation fresh flowers provide. Some clients may be hesitant towards tearing or cutting parts of the flower, so close observation and facial acceptance may be necessary. In groups allow members to decide together on the center and then take turns adding to the mandala. Flowers are very powerful symbols of major life events, so be prepared for heightened feelings while creating. This mandala is not dismantled by nature since the flowers were not found outside.

Discussion questions remain the same with the following additions:
- **What senses did you notice while creating this mandala?**
- **Did the flowers bring forth any memories for you?**

Floral Mandala

(Self created during a break between clients. I have found creating mandalas after difficult client sessions can be both soothing and energizing!)

Mandala #7

Name: Stone Mandala

Level: All ages and suitable for groups

Materials: Stones of various sizes/colors (can be collected on a nature walk or already in therapy room), folded sheet/large white paper/sand tray, permanent marker

Procedure:

Follow Step #1. Explain how the earliest mandalas in North America were found as stones arranged in a particular order and may have been used for rituals. Discuss how stones can often times help us feel grounded and focused when we hold them. Invite the client to go on a "Stone Walk" or have a variety of stones ready in the therapy room. Discuss the importance of the center stone (bindu), and allow the client to first pick which stone looks and feels like the perfect center for the mandala (Allow the child to not just look at stones, but to also hold, rub, shake, balance and even smell and listen to them them in an effort to allow a multi sensory experience. It might be a fun experience to have the client recline and place a stone on the tummy so he/she can make the stone move with the breath). Once the client has picked the bindu stone have the client begin creating the mandala. Remind the client to focus first on the center and then move outwards. Let him/her know that you will remain quiet during the creation, and to please let you know when finished by telling you or ringing the gong. Begin by ringing the gong.

Discussion:

I have recently added a new dimension to this intervention which has had a profound effect on the clients. During the processing questions, I added the final question: "Think about any of the difficulties you have had this past week, then think of a special word or symbol that could help you during this time." Most clients quite easily come up with a word that they believe could have helped them (a mantra of sorts). I then invite them to write that word on the center stone; the very stone they took such time and care to choose. This bindu then goes home with them as a reminder that they have the inner strength to maintain during difficult times.

Stone Mandala

(Completed by 10 year old boy titled "Happy". He was very excited to get to bring home the middle stone (It says "happy"). Little gifts can mean a lot to a child!

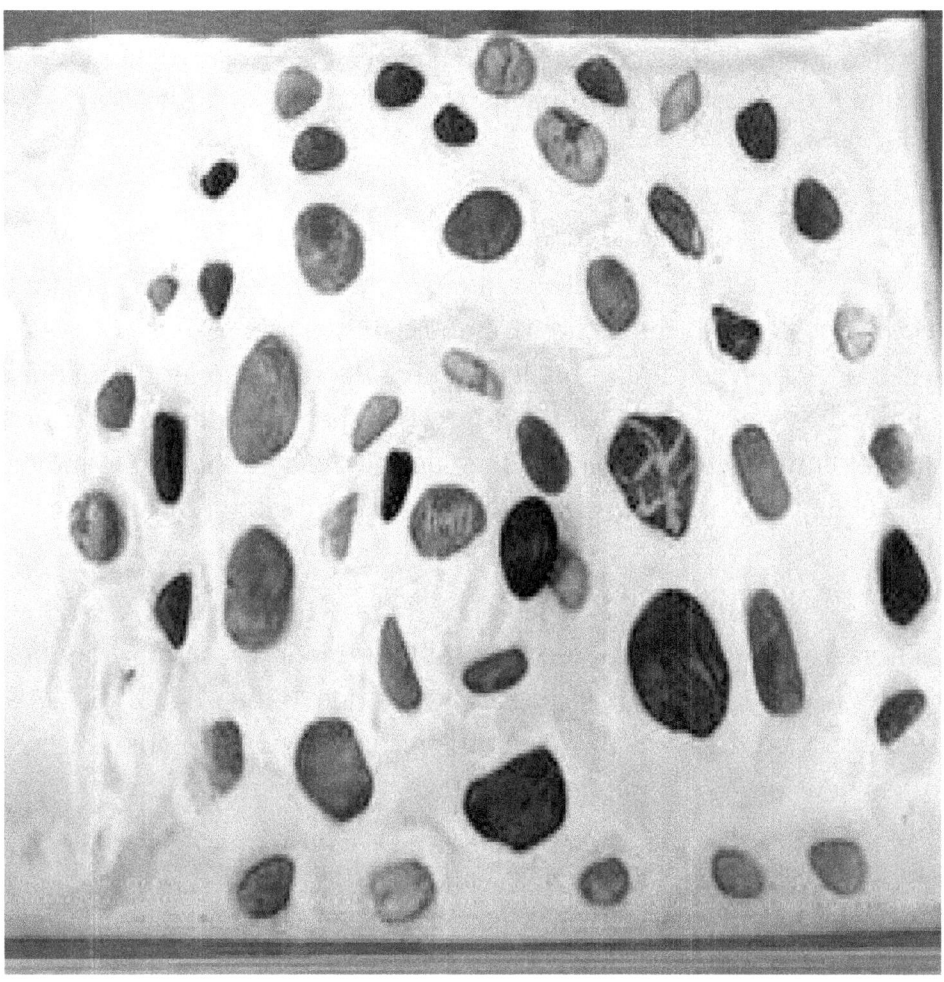

Mandala #8

Name: Special People Mandala

Level: Ages 3 and up and groups

Materials: Mandala template, pencil, crayons, markers, glue, scissors, copies of photos provided by families and/or guardians that can be cut up (optional)

Procedure:
Follow Step #1. Hand the client the mandala template and tell them today we are going to think of special people in his/her life. These are people who help them, care for them and love them no matter what. Give the client a minute or two to close his/her eyes and think of these special people. When finished tell the client to create a mandala of these special people using words, shapes, symbols or pictures. The client decides how best to represent these people. Remind the client of your silence during the creation and to indicate completion by telling you or ringing the gong. Begin by ringing the gong.

Discussion:
This intervention can be a wonderful reminder of the support clients have in their lives. Clients often feel isolated, unloved, and/or unlovable due to their behaviors, so this helps them realize the support they actually have. Clients typically like to bring this mandala home to post somewhere as a reminder of the love they have in their lives.

Discussion questions remain the same with the following addition:
- **After detailing each special person is there a way you can show them how you support and love them as well?**

Mandala #9

Name: Puzzle Mandala

Level: All ages, and is suitable for groups

Materials: Blank circle puzzle (several sizes are available at teacher stores or online), markers, one piece of child's favorite color construction paper

Procedure:
Follow Step #1. Discuss how early ancient mandalas were made one piece at a time, much like a puzzle. Have one piece of construction paper (child's favorite color) with all of the puzzle pieces on it. (Puzzle should be unassembled). Tell child to create colors, words, symbols, patterns on each puzzle piece. Explain that there is no wrong way to do this, and to create whatever feels right to him/her. Remind the client of your silence during the creation and to indicate completion by telling you or ringing the gong. Begin by ringing the gong. When client is completed assemble the pieces to discover the mandala that has been created.

In a group, the pieces can be split among group members, then follow the same procedure.

Discussion:
When I originally created this intervention I had the puzzle already assembled. I noticed that children would often get frustrated with this because the ridges in the puzzle would often affect their creations. On a whim I decided to try the intervention as described above, and it proved to be amazing! The suspense at where each piece will go causes much excitement with children, and they love discovering what the mandala looks like. One child said it best when she whispered, "Oh, it's magical!"

This intervention tends to be more vocal since the children often like to explain what and why they are creating each piece the way they are. I completely accept and track their words but do not add any additional conversation or insight. I do, however, process in the end how life can often be like a puzzle mandala; all the pieces of our lives may not feel important, but, when the whole picture is discovered it's magical!

Puzzle Mandala

(This mandala was created by an 8 year old boy titled "My Loves")

(This mandala was created by a 13 year old girl. She remained quiet while creating, and was very introspective throughout the creation.

Mandala #10

Name: Miniature Mandala

Level: All ages and suitable for groups

Materials: Sand tray, miniatures

Procedure:
Follow Step #1. Reiterate how the center of the mandala (the bindu) is the most sacred, important part to the creator. Instruct child to observe all of the miniatures in the room, and pick the one that is the most powerful or sacred to him/her. Give the child time to complete this. Have the child place this chosen miniature in the center of the sand. Then allow child to create one, two, or three more concentric circles around the bindu, using his/her finger. When this is done, instruct the child to pick additional miniatures to place around these circles. There is no wrong way to do this. Any number of miniatures can be used; this is completely up to the child. Remind the client of your silence during the creation and to indicate completion by telling you or ringing the gong. Begin by ringing the gong.

Discussion:
A sand tray and miniatures are obviously needed for this intervention. Many children especially love the multi-sensory component of this mandala. One frequent mandala creator stated he liked that it was "3-D".

For younger clients, I may become a bit more direct and sequential to help them understand the creation better. For example, I can tell them to first pick the sacred miniature, then 4-6 special miniatures to place around the first circle in the sand, then 8-10 special miniatures for the second circle, etc.

Processing this mandala can be very insightful since often the clients are picking items that may initially seem unrelated to each other. The items also tend to have deep significance to them as well. Make sure to ask children to tell a story about the mandala; I have heard some beautiful stories when using this intervention.

Miniature Mandala

(This mandala was created by an 11 year old client. The creation has additional features of "scary" miniatures outside of the mandala. Notice also, there is a bridge connected the mandala to the outside; much like one of the four doors in Hindu and Buddhist mandalas.)

Mandala #11

Name: Check-in Mandala

Level: Ages three and up, as well as groups

Materials: Mandala template, pencil, crayons, markers

Procedure:
Follow Step #1. Have the client take a minute or two to think about all of the things that have happened in his/her life since the last therapy session. Focus on different feelings/emotions that have been experienced. When finished, hand the client the mandala template and explain that this will be a check-in mandala. The client may choose to fill the mandala with any words, shapes, symbols or pictures that summarize how things have been since the last session. In the center of the mandala (the bindu) the client may choose one word, shape or symbol that sums up the experiences. Remind the client of your silence during the creation and to indicate completion by telling you or ringing the gong. Begin by ringing the gong.

Discussion:
As most of us in the helping profession know, simply asking the question, "How have you been?" or "What has been going on since I last saw you", will lead to many "Fine", "I don't remember" and "Nothing" responses. Art is a great way for the client to detail how things have been going without having to necessarily talk about it. Giving the client a few minutes to think about the time between visits does help jog the memory, but clients also remember things while creating the mandala. If clients truly can't remember anything that has happened I instruct them to use colors, shapes and symbols to help show the feelings they have experienced since the previous visit. This often helps them remember specific situations they wish to share. Check-in mandalas are also a wonderful tool to promote self-awareness and self-advocacy. Clients can create and use the check-in mandala to self-monitor and self-evaluate their progress towards reaching their therapeutic goals.

Discussion questions are the same with the following additions:
- **In looking at your mandala, what have you noticed about the past week/two weeks/month?**
- **Is there something new we should focus on after processing this mandala?**

Mandala #12

Name: Mantra Mandala

Level: Ages 6 and up, as well as groups

Materials: Mandala template, pencil, eraser, crayons, colored pencils, markers

Procedure:
Follow Step #1. Reiterate how the center of the mandala (the bindu) is the most sacred, important part to the creator. Discuss how we can often think of one (or a few) words that perfectly describe what we are currently experiencing. Have the client take several quiet moments to think about what he/she has been feeling, thinking, and experiencing lately in life. Ask them to imagine one word (or a few, if needed) to help define this experience. Then give the client the paper mandala and have them draw a circle in the center, and place his/her word in the center. Explain that the rest of the mandala can be any pictures, symbols or words to help further explain the chosen word. Color may be used if wanted. Remind the client of your silence during the creation and to indicate completion by telling you or ringing the gong. Begin by ringing the gong.

Discussion:
This intervention helps clarify the often chaotic and overwhelming thoughts and feelings clients may experience. Clients might feel stuck as a result of "negative" emotions and thoughts, and they will often pick one of these feelings or emotions as their center word. Choosing one word helps to tune into what is occurring at that moment. Additional words/symbols/pictures help to process and further clarify possible solutions to the issue. This intervention allows for both cognitive and artistic exploration.

Discussion questions remain the same with the following additions:
- What do you notice about your current situation after viewing this mandala?
- What is one thing you can change to help you in this situation?

Mantra Mandala

(Created by Pre-Licensed counselor under my professional supervision. Often times supervision sessions can be enhanced with art and play techniques. Supervision can be a very stressful time in a person's life, so processing this is essential).

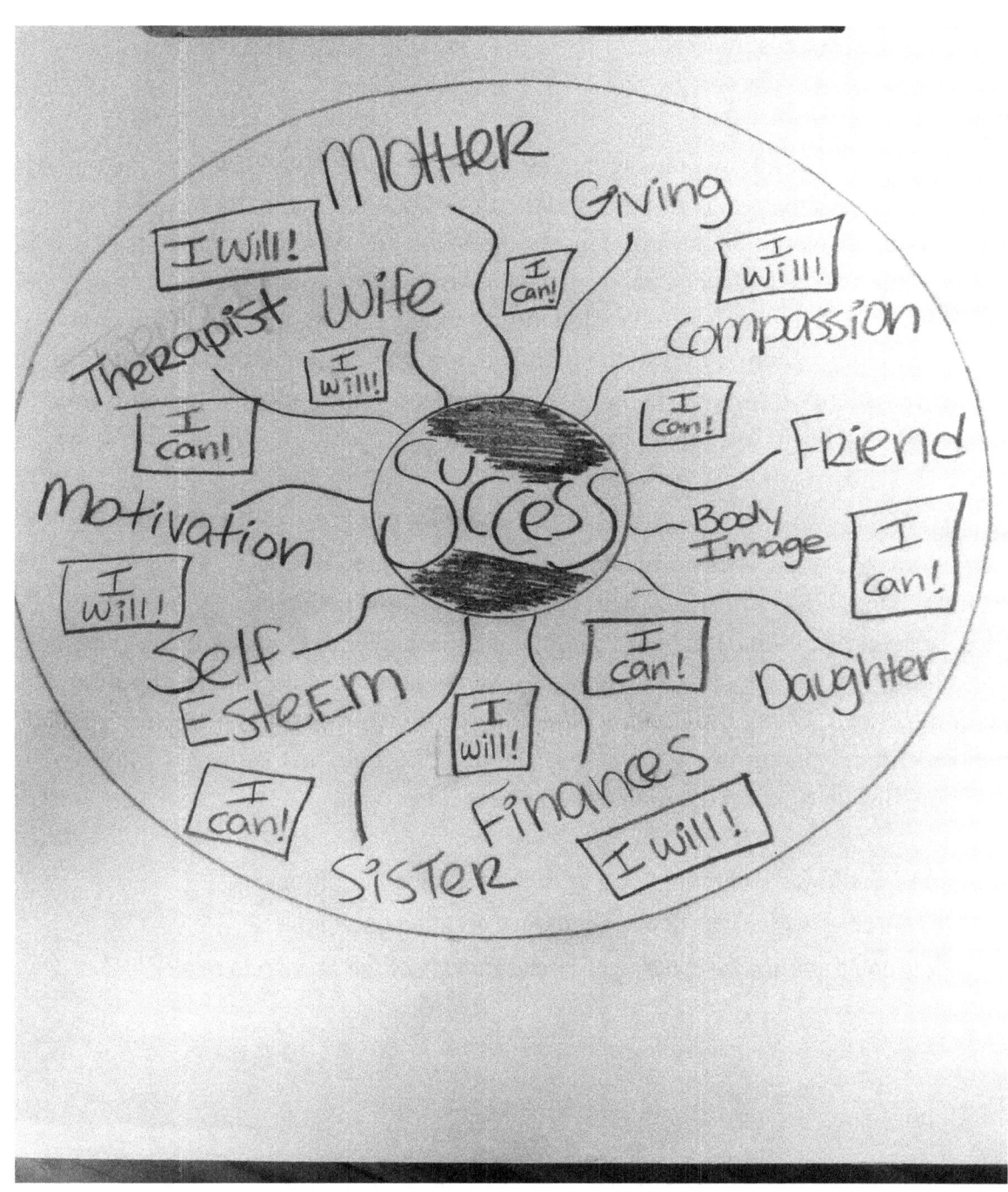

Mandala #13

Name: Circle Mandala

Level: Ages 6 and up as well as groups

Materials: Mandala template, compass, circle stencil template, pencil, eraser, **Optional:** crayons, colored pencils, markers

Procedure:
Follow Step #1. Explain how drawing circles can be relaxing. Give the client the mandala template and direct them to create a mandala of his/her choice initially by only creating circles. These circles can be any size, and created with any writing instruments he/she chooses. There can be a few circles, or many circles; there is no wrong way to complete the mandala. Once the circles are created the client can choose to color them, write words or symbols in them, or finish the mandala however he/she wishes. Remind the client of your silence during the creation and to indicate completion by telling you or ringing the gong. Begin by ringing the gong.

Discussion:
I have discovered that clients complete this in a wide variety of ways. The circles may be created by hand, or very precisely with a compass or stencil. Clients may overlap the circles, or keep them separate. Some circle mandalas have many circles of various sizes, while others have had very few, in equal size. Many of my younger clients choose to color each of the circles, where some of my older clients use words to help process particular situations currently occurring in their lives. The less directive the therapist is while explaining this intervention the more creative it will become!

Discussion questions remain the same with the following additions:
- Tell me different feelings you noticed while creating your circles.
- How could you use the drawing of circles outside of the session to relax?

Circle Mandala

(Circle Mandala completed by 11 year old client who had previously been given strategies for Executive Function difficulties. He created larger circles to represent interventions he feels will work best. Photo blurry to protect client details.)

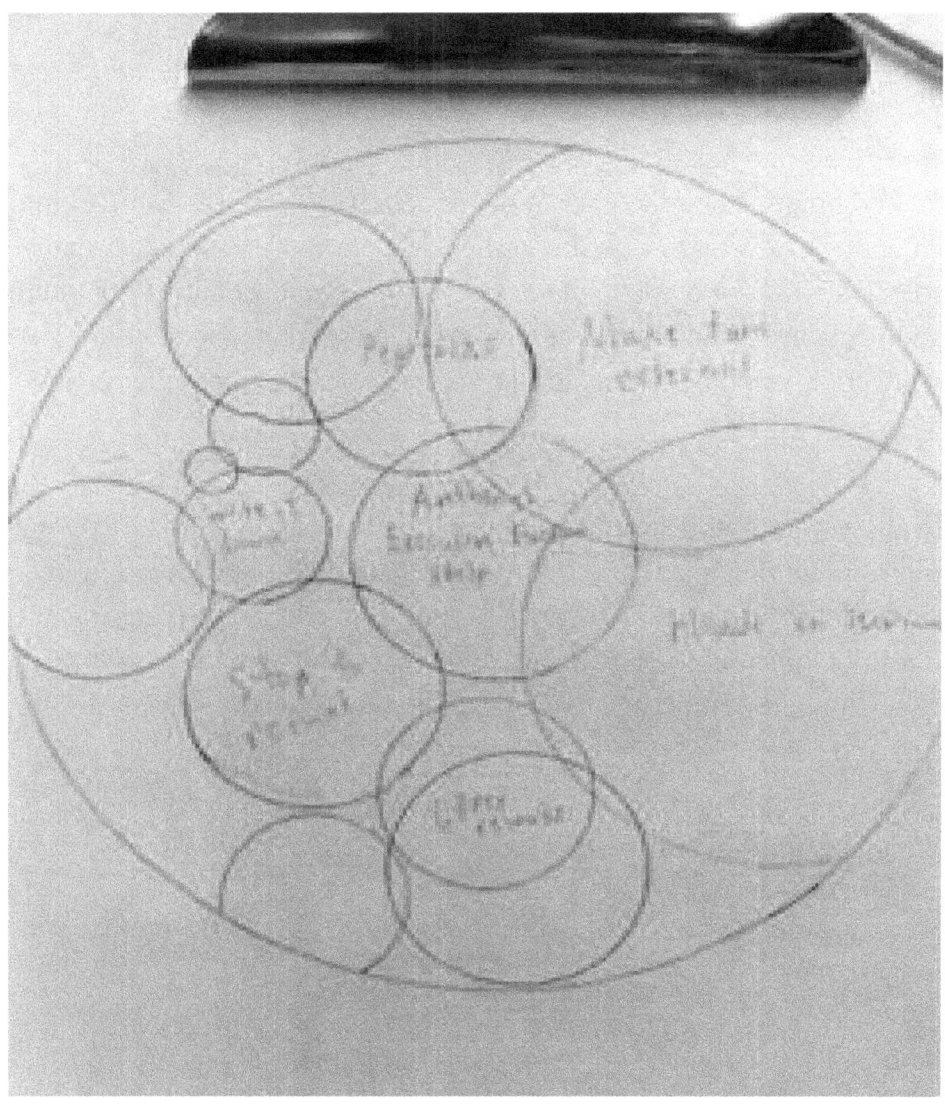

Mandala #14

Name: Gem Mandala

Level: All ages and groups

Materials: Mandala template, plastic gem jewels (self adhesive work best), glue (if using gems without adhesive)

Procedure:
Follow Step #1. Describe how many ancient mandalas found in churches and temples are very colorful and bright. Hand the child the mandala template and instruct him/her to fill the mandala with whatever gems he/she wishes. He/she can use however many gems in whatever colors needed to complete the artwork. The gem most appealing to him/her can be placed in the center as the bindu. Remind the client of your silence during the creation and to indicate completion by telling you or ringing the gong. Begin by ringing the gong.

Discussion:
This activity allows clients to use a different medium for mandala creation, while creating similar results to traditional mandalas. Many clients who do not enjoy coloring, or who have fine motor difficulties holding a crayon find this activity more pleasant. Therapists do not want to restrict the amount of gems used, however if a thousand gems are placed before some clients, a thousand gems will be used! I tend to place about fifty gems of various colors and sizes at our creative space and this seems to be a good number to offer. In group settings clients may work together to create the mandala, or each client can take a turn adding one gem to the mandala.

Gem Mandala

(Created by a 5 year old client. Titled "Shiny New")

Mandala #15

Name: Cardinal Direction Mandala

Level: Ages eight and up

Materials: Mandala template on following page, pencil, crayons, markers, colored pencils

Procedure:
Follow Step #1. Briefly describe that in ancient Celtic symbolism, the four directions were believed to symbolize the growth, passions, emotions and security experienced by individuals and communities. These four areas can be important to understand about ourselves as well. How secure do we currently feel? What are things that excite us and spark our passion? What emotions have we been experiencing? What growth have we had, or wish to have? These are all deep and thought provoking questions. Hand the client the mandala template on the following page and have them fill in the mandala with shapes, colors, words and pictures that help them answer these questions. The client may want to use the north, south, west and east format to detail each area, or he/she may wish to combine the four areas into one composite piece of art. It is the client's choice to creatively consider these qualities and decide how to express them. Remind the client of your silence during the creation and to indicate completion by telling you or ringing the gong. Begin by ringing the gong.

Discussion:
A great deal of insight may be discovered after completing this intervention. I have found this intervention works better with clients older than eight, who have been in therapy for some time with me. I would not do this intervention early on, but rather after we have had some successes in meeting client goals. That way they will be able to artistically process and document their growth as well as additional safety needs yet to be met and still in progress. This intervention seems to create a longer amount of processing time, so be prepared to spend the entire session on this. This intervention can also be used as a fantastic tool for goal setting!

Process using all of the questions found in Chapter 7.

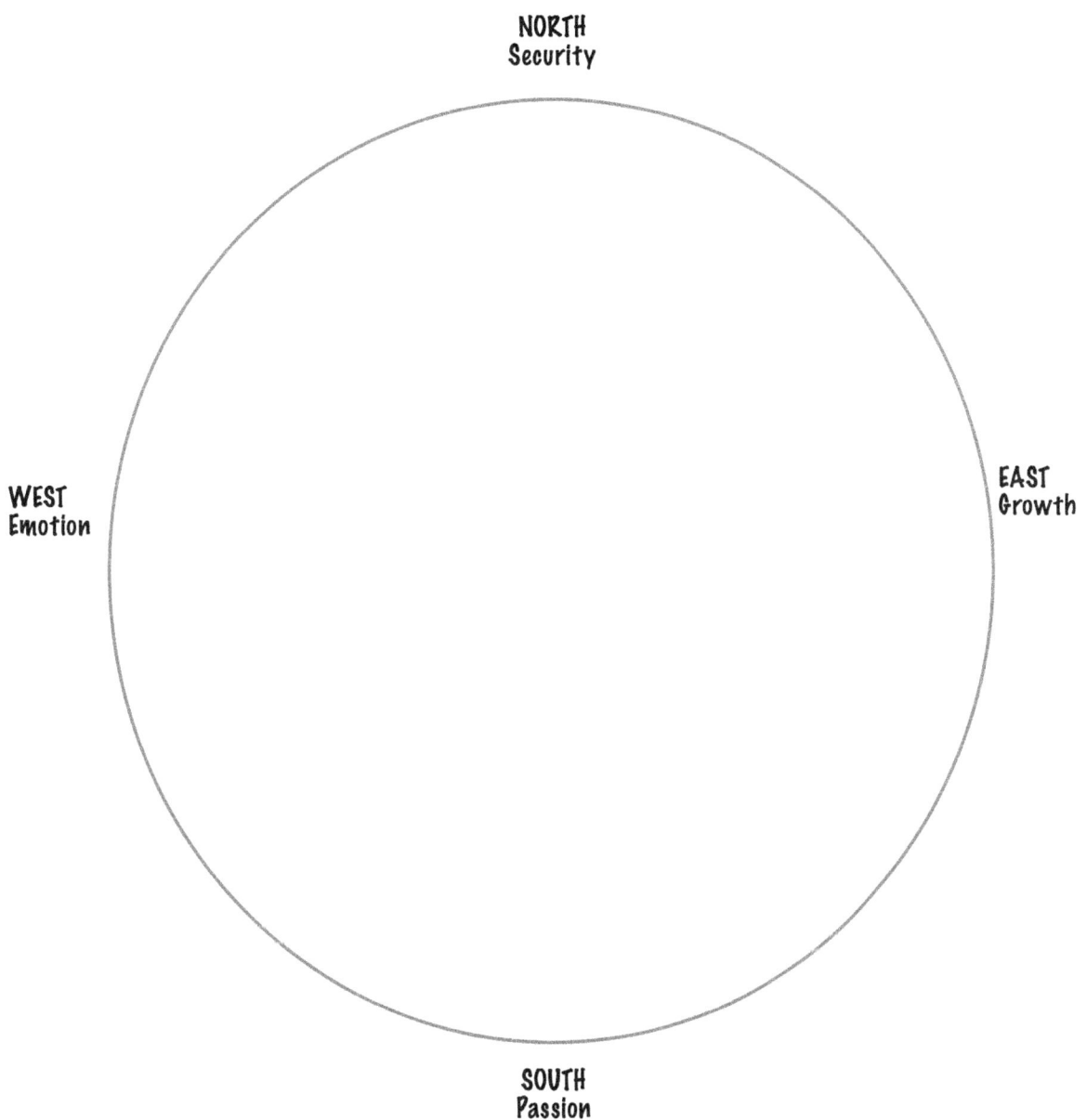

Mandala #16

Name: Confetti Mandala

Level: Ages 6 and up

Materials: Mandala template, glitter glue, hole punch, multi color construction paper, paint brush, crayons, colored pencils, markers, envelope, place mat or table cloth

Procedure:
Follow Step #1. Explain how confetti is a fun way to create artwork, and that we will be making our own confetti to complete the mandala. Allow the child to pick construction paper colors, and to use the hole punch to create the confetti. Place the confetti in an envelope until ready to use. When complete, place the mandala template on the place mat or table cloth and instruct the child to "paint the mandala" using glitter glue and a paint brush. When finished, explain to the child that he/she will now take the confetti and toss it onto the mandala freely. We are not looking for perfection; instead we are tossing the confetti as we would at a party and allowing it to land wherever it chooses. Remind the client of your silence during the creation and to indicate completion by telling you or ringing the gong. Begin by ringing the gong.

Discussion:
As one may possibly guess, this is a very fun and often not quiet mandala creation session! The clients love the opportunity to paint using glue and haphazardly throwing confetti. This intervention can be very freeing for the client who needs things ordered and detailed. I find it very important to connect this activity to real life by using the metaphor of life often being "out of our hands" as the confetti was. However, it may still turn out to be beautiful.

Discussion questions remain the same with the following addition:
- **What do you feel like you don't have control over in your life, and how can this be viewed as a positive/beautiful thing?**

Confetti Mandala

(Created by 9 year old client. She chose to only put glue around her bindu so it would remain "clean". Sacred center is cross and "nice spot that is on Indian people". The confetti processed as all of the uncontrollable things in her life that bother her, but keep her center strong.)

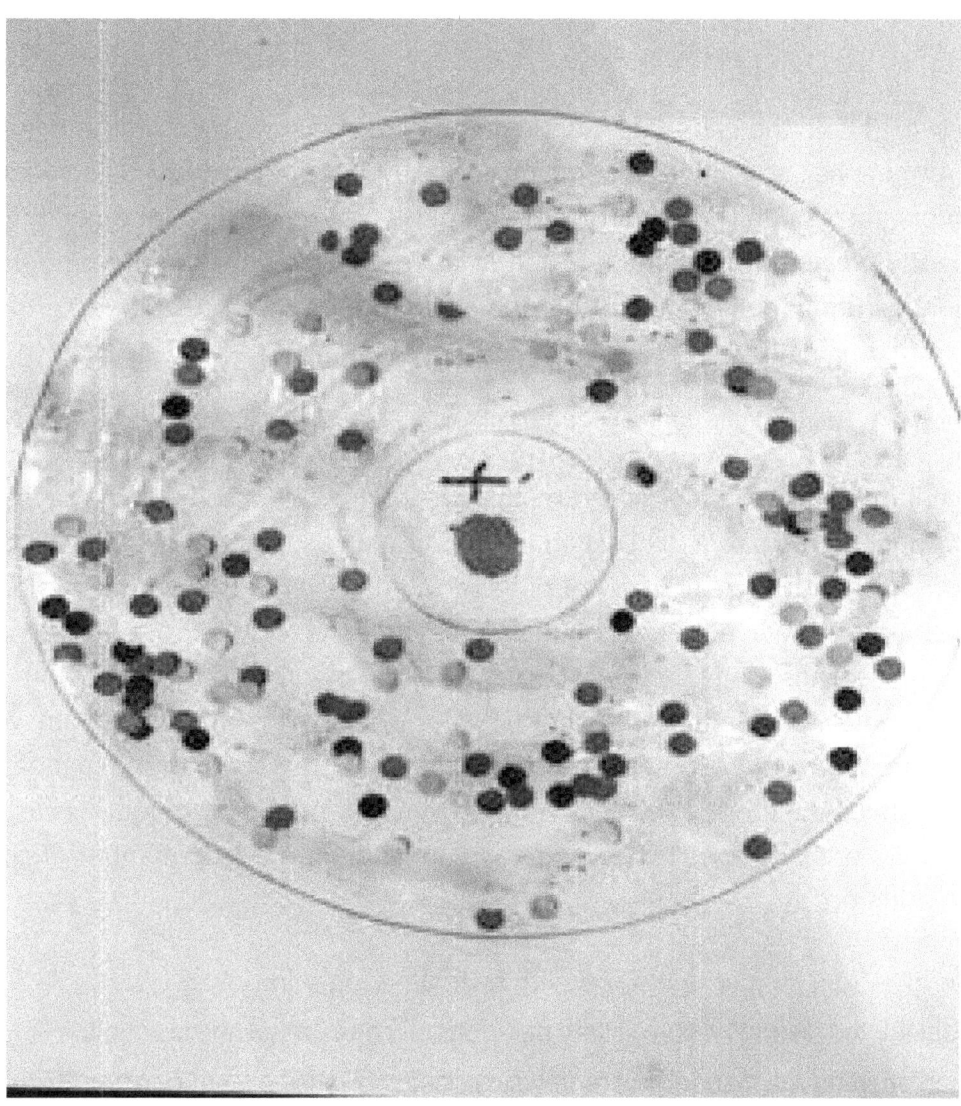

Mandala #17

Name: Folded Mandala

Level: Ages 6 and up

Materials: Mandala template (thicker construction paper works best), pencil, paints, paint brushes, cup of water, paper towels, markers

Procedure:
Follow Step #1. Hand the client the mandala template and have them fold the circle in half. Explain how he/she will be painting one half of the mandala only, using whatever shapes, colors and designs he/she chooses. Tell how the mandala will then be folded in half and lightly pressed, then opened to see what artwork was created. Remind the client of your silence during the creation and to indicate completion by telling you or ringing the gong. Begin by ringing the gong.

Discussion:
This intervention allows for free, non-directive creating, while also having a surprising finished product for the client. Clients are often more focused and quiet during this intervention, as they attempt to keep all of their painting on one half of the mandala. They tend to use great care when folding the mandala, and receive an extra sensory experience by pressing their hands along their masterpieces, achieving a work of art on both halves. Imagine the great surprise and excitement when re-opening their mandalas! I have noticed that most of the time there remains a spot of white along the center of the mandala. When this occurs, I invite the client to write a word, symbol, or picture with markers as a personal mantra of their work. I have seen many beautiful and deep mantras created from this simple addition.

Discussion questions remain the same with the following additions:
- Describe the feelings involved with painting only one half of the mandala.
- When opening the mandala were you surprised? Describe what you now see?
- What word/picture/shape can you put in the center of your mandala to help you with your upcoming week/month?

Folded Mandala

(Completed by 12 year old client. Paint is showing what her anxiety feels like to her; center stating "I'm o.k."

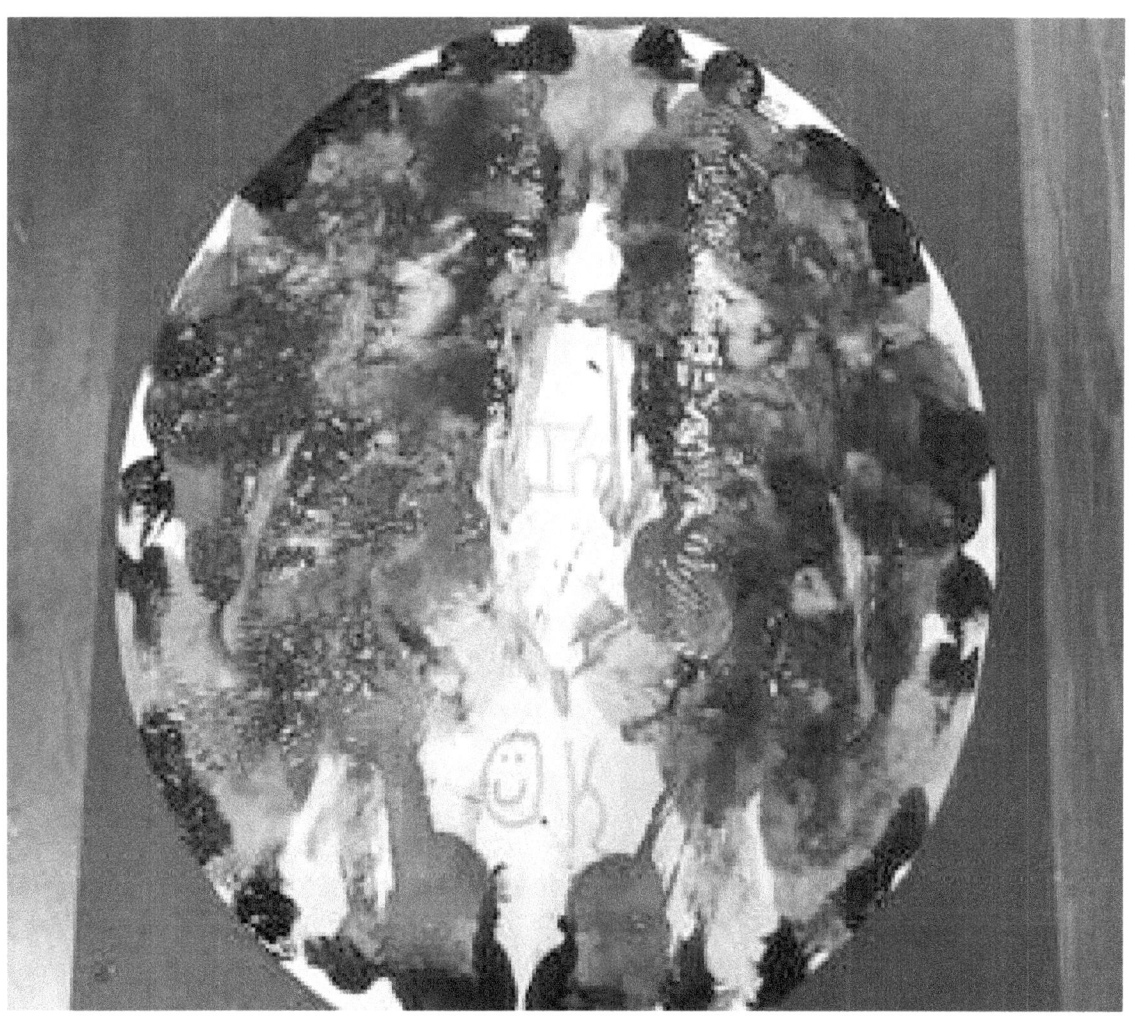

Mandala #18

Name: Linear Mandala

Levels: All ages

Materials: Mandala template, pencil, eraser, markers, ruler, crayons, colored pencils

Procedure:
Follow Step #1. Hand the client the mandala template and explain that they are to make lines using the ruler or free-hand lines throughout the mandala. Welcome them to make as many or as few lines as they wish using a pencil, and then coloring in with crayons, markers or colored pencils. Remind the client of your silence during the creation and to indicate completion by telling you or ringing the gong. Begin by ringing the gong.

Discussion:
As discussed in Chapter 4, drawing lines has the ability to bring clients back to their younger years of exploration with scribbling. Lines can help clients feel peaceful, focused, or expressive of anxiety and fear. Often times I can process quietly the clients' internal psychological state just by observing them during the creation process. The darkness of the lines drawn, the intensity in which the hand is drawing them, and the jagged or uniform pattern of the lines often indicate how the clients are feeling, and help guide me to dig a bit deeper during the processing phase.

Additional discussion questions may include:
- **Did you notice different feelings from these lines versus these lines? (Comparing two different types of lines)**

Linear Mandala

(Created by 12 year old client, titled "Stress")

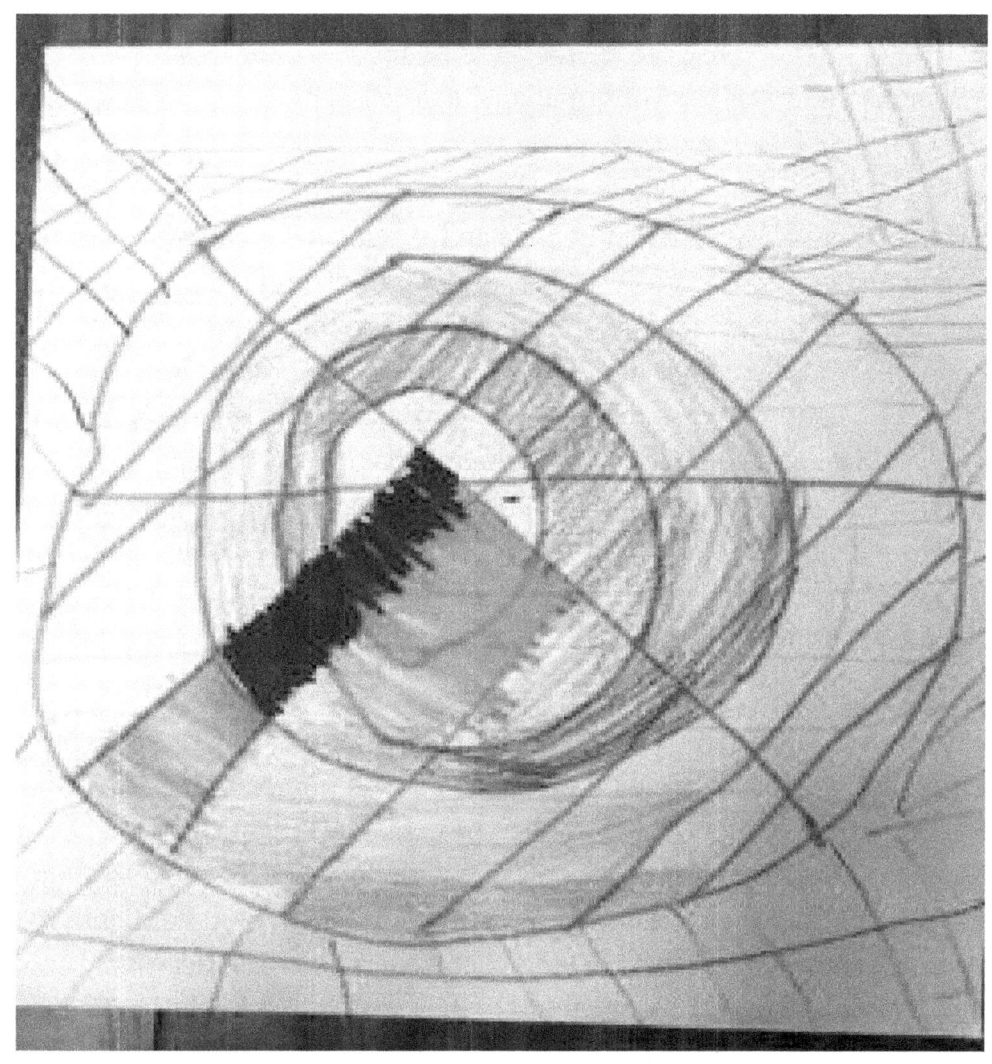

Mandala #19

Name: One Color Mandala

Level: All ages

Materials: Mandala template, crayons, markers, colored pencils

Procedure:
Follow Step #1. Discuss how different colors can have special meaning for us, and we may identify a particular feeling to a color. Have the client think about the feelings he/she has experienced lately, then have him/her choose one feeling that stands out. Allow client to pick one color that most identifies that feeling. It is possible for the client to pick multiple shades of the color chosen, or use different mediums of the chosen color. Hand the client the mandala template and guide them to fill the mandala with any shapes, symbols, words or pictures using just the chosen color. Remind the client of your silence during the creation and to indicate completion by telling you or ringing the gong. Begin by ringing the gong.

Discussion:
This intervention helps the therapist and client tune in and focus on one specific emotion the client is feeling. Choosing to create the mandala with one color may help clients more deeply feel the primary emotion that has been present. The therapist should pay attention to how the clients are creating; are they coloring with light or dark strokes? Multiple shades or one shade? Are they holding their instrument with intensity or lightly? How does their expression look while creating? Do the clients seem to create decisively and deliberately or impulsively and chaotically? Do they seem thoughtful, intuitive, hyper-aroused or calm? Do they work quickly or slowly?

Discussion questions may remain the same with the following additions:
- Which feeling were you displaying in your creation?
- What about the color _____ reminds you of this feeling?
- Does the act of creating with this color seem to soothe or magnify the feeling?

Mandala #20

Name: Labyrinth Mandala

Level: Ages four and up

Materials: Wood circle (found at craft stores), pictures of labyrinths, sand, glitter, wood glue, pencil

Procedure:
Discuss how labyrinths have been used to help people focus and relax. Explain how today's mandala will be a handheld labyrinth to help the client relax. Hand the client the wood template and have them create a wavy, connected line using the pencil. Remind the client not to make the design too narrow because the glue will be used to trace over the pencil design. When the pencil design is completed, have the client trace over it with the glue. Place the wood circle over a tray of sand and/or glitter, and have the client sprinkle the sand/glitter onto the wood. Lightly shake off the excess sand and/or glitter, and allow to dry for at least twelve hours before using.

Discussion:
Most clients will need some help with this activity since it needs to be completed in steps. It may not be feasible for the therapist to be silent during the process of this mandala, but quiet is encouraged while the client is creating the pencil design and adding the glue. It is important to remind the client not to use this handheld labyrinth for at least twelve hours, otherwise the sand/glitter may not stick. This has been a popular intervention with many of my clients, and the parents have expressed that it is used at home quite a bit! With younger clients, or those new to the labyrinth, demonstrate how to use your finger or a stylus to "walk" the labyrinth, tracing the path to the center, pausing to breathe, and then using your finger to "walk" your way out through the curves and turns.

Labyrinth Mandala

(Created by 10 year old client titled "Maze")

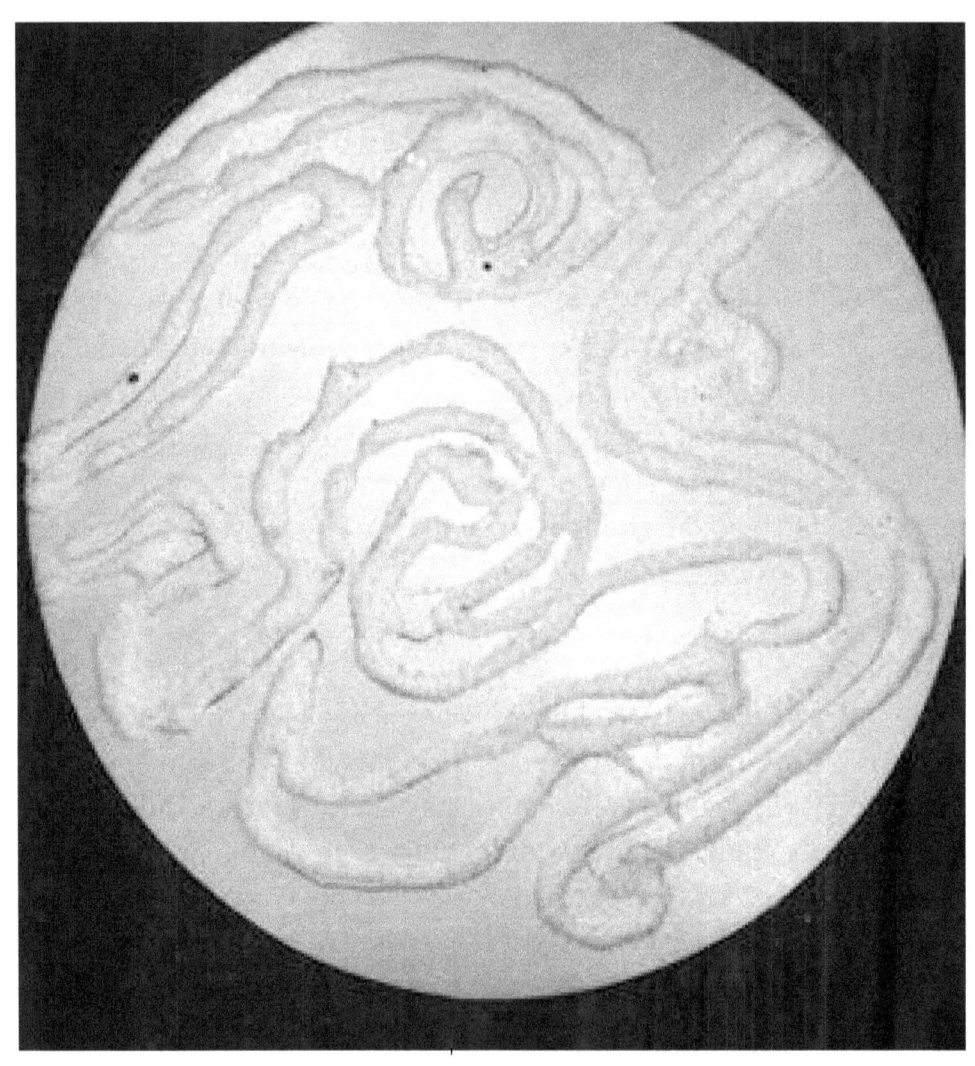

Mandala #21

Name: Number Mandala

Level: All ages

Materials: Mandala template, pencil, crayons, markers, colored pencils

Procedure:
Follow Step #1. Explain how many ancient mandalas contain numbers that have particular spiritual significance. Invite the client to choose two or three numbers that are personally significant to use in his/her masterpiece. Hand the client the mandala template and explain that he/she should fill the mandala with the chosen numbers. These numbers can be any size, shape, or color, and can be used as many times as needed for the client. Remind the client of your silence during the creation and to indicate completion by telling you or ringing the gong. Begin by ringing the gong.

Discussion:
Numbers can have particular significance to clients, and they typically choose numbers quite easily. Clients who don't feel artistic find this mandala less threatening and easier to complete. It is amazing to me how often numbers have been enhanced to make other shapes and symbols! Clients may choose to color this mandala, however many use the time to focus on manipulating the numbers and do not color it.

Additional discussion questions may include:
- **Tell me about the numbers you chose for your artwork.**
- **Tell me how you decided to use more of (this number) than of (that number).**

Number Mandala

(Created by 15 year old client, titled "15")

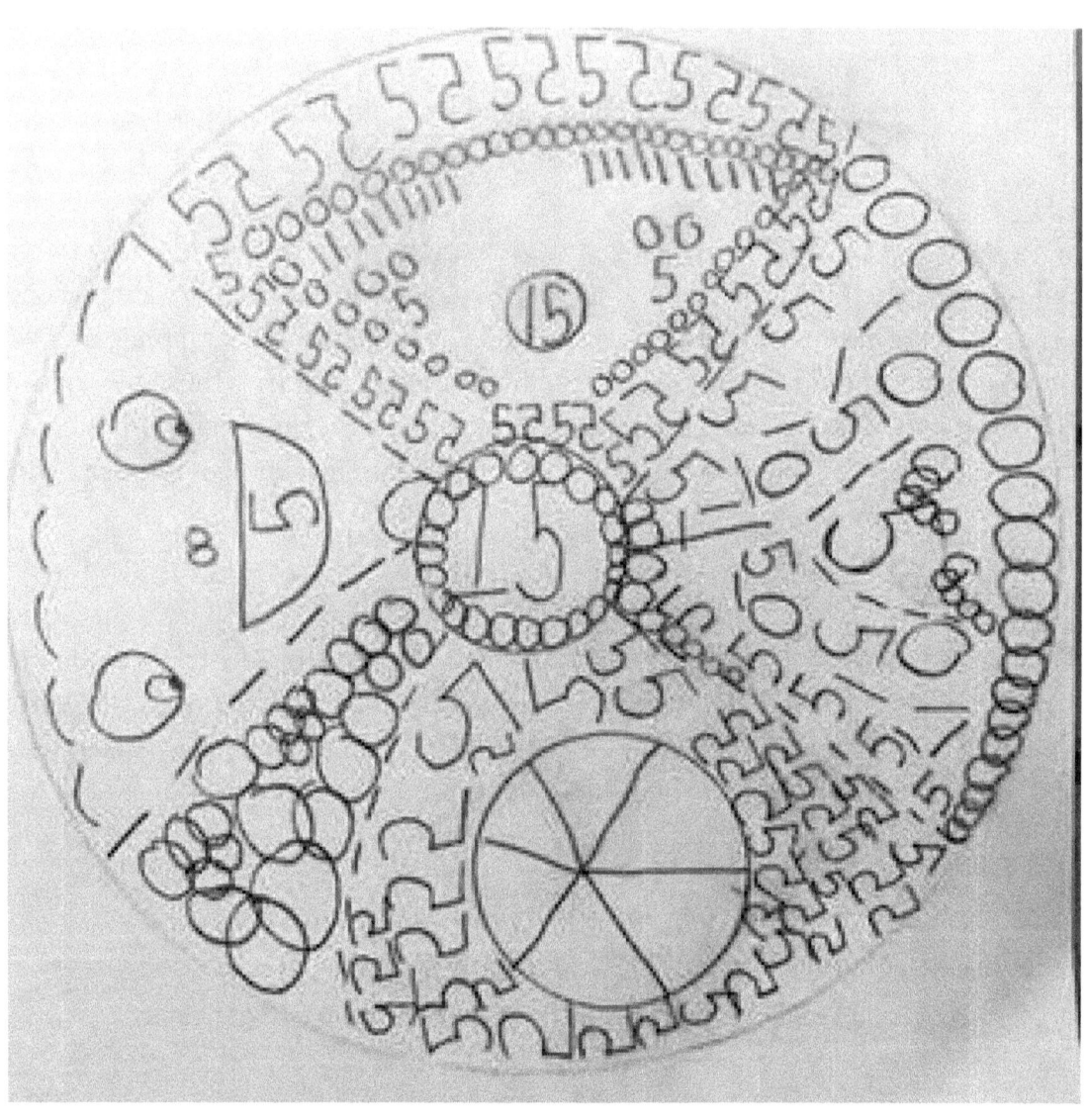

Mandala #22

Name: Feelings Mandala

Level: All ages and groups

Materials: Mandala template, pencil, crayons, markers, colored pencils

Procedure:
Follow Step #1. Discuss how we may have many feelings throughout our week, some more often than others. Have the client think about what feelings he/she has been experiencing this week and which emotions have been felt the strongest. Hand the client the mandala template and explain that he/she can make as many concentric circles needed within the template. Invite the client to create a heart in the center circle. Next, have the client write the feeling felt the most in the circle closest to the heart. Each subsequent feeling can be written on the next circle in relation to how often it has been experienced. When completed, invite client to color each concentric circle using the color that symbolizes the particular feeling.

Discussion:
This mandala intervention is sequential, so complete silence by the therapist may not be possible. I keep concentric circle templates handy for those clients who prefer to use a guide instead of creating these on their own. For younger clients the therapist will need to explain one step at a time to ensure the client grasps the directive. Older clients may be able to complete this quietly without continuous instruction. This mandala helps clients organize their feelings and process possible reasons for the feelings. Adding color to the mandala helps the therapist discover the particular meaning attached to the colors chosen for the emotion.

Feelings Mandala

(Created by 5 year old client, titled "My Heart")

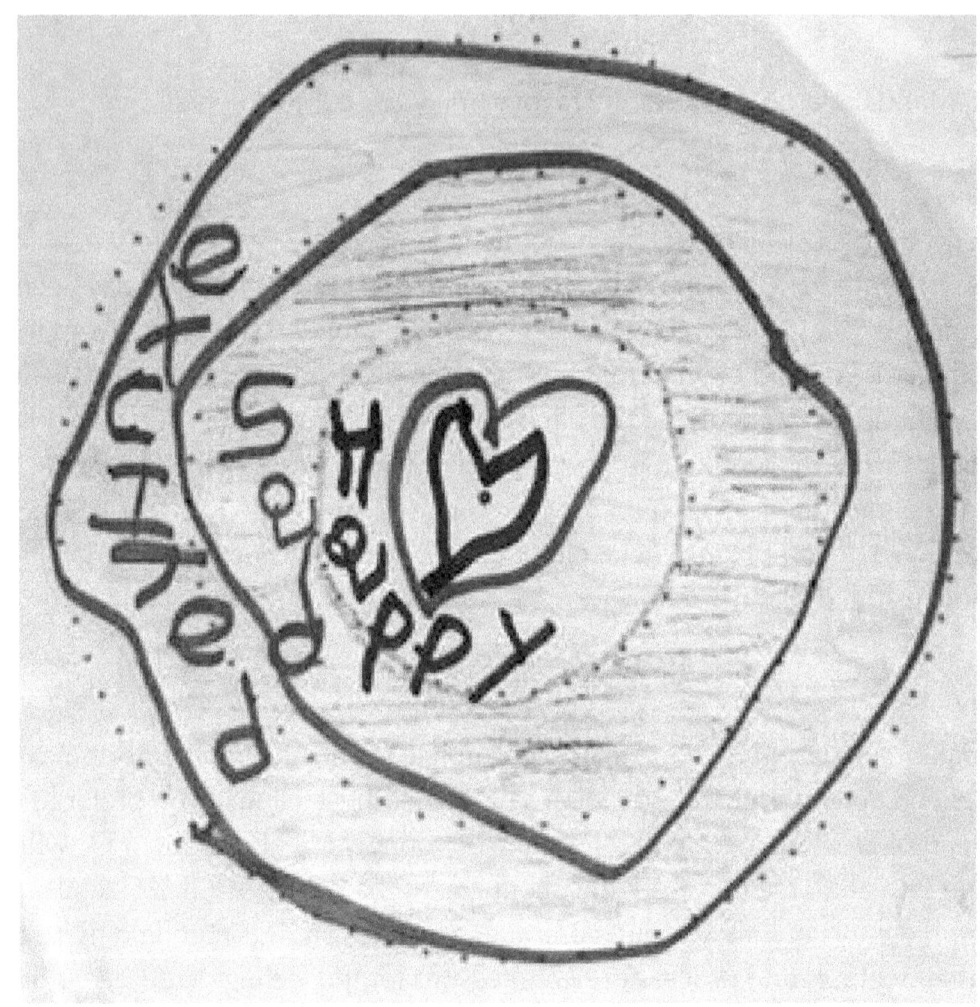

Mandala #23

Name: Scribble Mandala

Level: Ages three and up

Materials: Mandala template, pencil, crayons, markers, colored pencils

Procedure:
Follow Step #1. Discuss how our first pieces of art as toddlers were scribble drawings, and how creating scribbles helped us focus and feel successful. Hand the client the mandala template and instruct him/her to free draw scribbles in whatever way feels comfortable. The client should fill the entire mandala with scribbles. When finished, tell the client he/she can color in whatever shapes/designs were created from the scribbles. Remind the client of your silence during the creation and to indicate completion by telling you or ringing the gong. Begin by ringing the gong.

Discussion:
Scribble mandalas are yet another intervention that can free clients from believing that their artwork must look a specific way. Scribble mandalas can help clients experiment with color, and find a multitude of shapes and designs within their scribble art. This intervention typically leads to a lot of laughter, and is a great relaxation tool to use throughout the course of therapy.

Use processing questions from Chapter 7.

Mandala #24

Name: Wellness Mandala

Level: Ages ten and up as well as groups

Materials: Types of Health sheet (on following page), mandala template, pencil, crayons, markers, colored pencils

Procedure:
Discuss the importance of health and balance in one's life. Describe how often we focus too heavily on one aspect of our health, while ignoring other areas. Hand the client the Types of Health sheet and discuss the different types of health. Allow client to add in any other types of health that are pertinent to his/her situation. When completed, have the client draw four lines to form a "pie" within the mandala. There should be eight wedges. (The therapist could have this completed ahead of time for younger clients). The client should then choose eight areas of health, writing in one for each piece of the mandala. At this point the therapist should ask the client to think about how balanced he/she is feeling in each of these areas. Starting at the center of the mandala, the client should color in how fully he/she is feeling balanced for each type of health. (The more a piece is colored, the more balanced the client is feeling.) Remind the client of your silence during the creation and to indicate completion by telling you or ringing the gong. Begin by ringing the gong.

Discussion:
This is one of my favorite interventions, so much so that I regularly complete it myself! It is a wonderful tool to visually see how balanced/unbalanced our lives currently are, and to then set goals towards greater health. Much of the discussion will focus on clients describing how much they colored in each component of health, and then sharing their reasoning for each area. I like to use the metaphor of a wheel with this mandala; if we have balanced and unbalanced pieces to our health we are not going to be able to flow smoothly, like an unbalanced wheel. When finished with the processing I often have the client write one goal on the back of the mandala to focus on during the week.

Types of Health
©Tracy Turner-Bumberry

Physical: Am I eating well, sleeping enough, exercising and balancing my school/work versus my leisure time?

Emotional: Am I taking care of, expressing and acknowledging my feelings; not trying to run from my feelings nor become too entrenched in them?

Mental: Am I making wise choices, weighing out all options and focusing on my needs? Am I able to think clearly and rationally?

Spiritual: Have I been active in my church/mosque/temple, or spent time praying/meditating/being in nature?

Social: Have I been balancing my social life; not spending too much or too little time with my friends?

Financial: Have I had extra money to treat myself, either through my allowance or my job?

Family: Have I been able to spend fun, quality time with my family; has my family been nurturing and supportive to each other?

Intellectual: Have I been spending enough time on my school studies or other intellectual pursuits?

- _____:
- _____:
- _____:

Wellness Mandala

(Created by 14 year old client titled "Wellness Wheel")

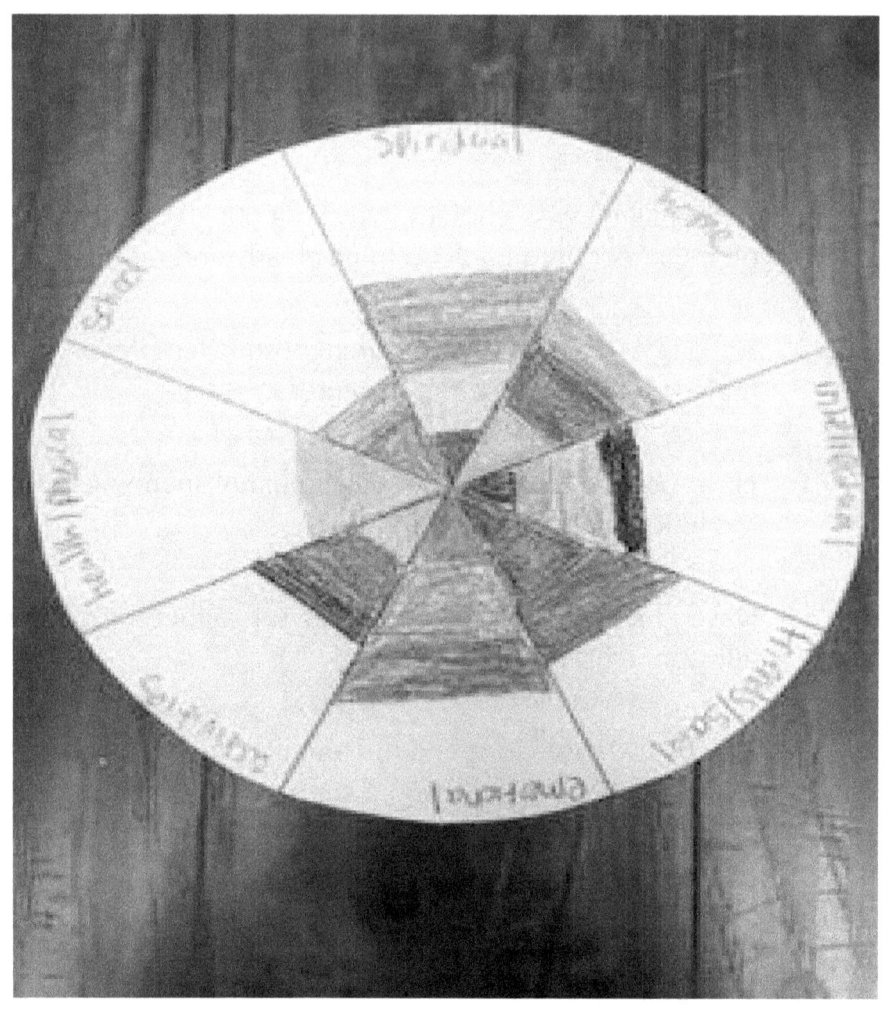

Mandala #25

Name: Multi-Media Mandala

Level: All Ages

Materials: Mandala template, crayons, markers, colored pencils, pastels, any craft materials available (I have duct tape, stickers, glitter, glitter glue, pom poms, pipe cleaners, gems, etc.)

Procedure:
Follow Step #1. Speak about how some mandalas were created by sand, while others were created with whatever materials were available, rocks, leaves, sticks, etc. Also discuss how many great artists use a variety of tools and mediums in which to create great masterpieces. Explain how today the client will choose whatever arts and crafts supplies he/she would like to create the mandala. There is no wrong way of completing this, advise to just choose whatever materials feel right and to fill the mandala however he/she chooses. Advise that any material that is out can be used, and it is up to the client to decide how much or how little to use on the mandala. Remind the client of your silence during the creation and to indicate completion by telling you or ringing the gong. Begin by ringing the gong.

Discussion:
This intervention allows for a great deal of freedom and expression from the client. Those clients who don't necessarily feel artistic will enjoy using other types of materials to create their mandalas. This is a non-directive mandala in that whatever they choose to use, whatever the topic, is completely up to them. I do advise therapists to offer the amount of each supply they are willing to give up in that particular session. Many clients may use every single bead that is laid out if given the opportunity! Wisely and purposely choose the number of each craft item you put in the art space before the client session begins. I also believe that five or six craft items, in addition to the coloring utensils is a good number of items to have for the client to use; too many choices may backfire and overwhelm the client.

Multi-Media Mandala

(Created by 11 year old client using paper, crayons, markers, gems and foam stickers. Titled "Dreams")

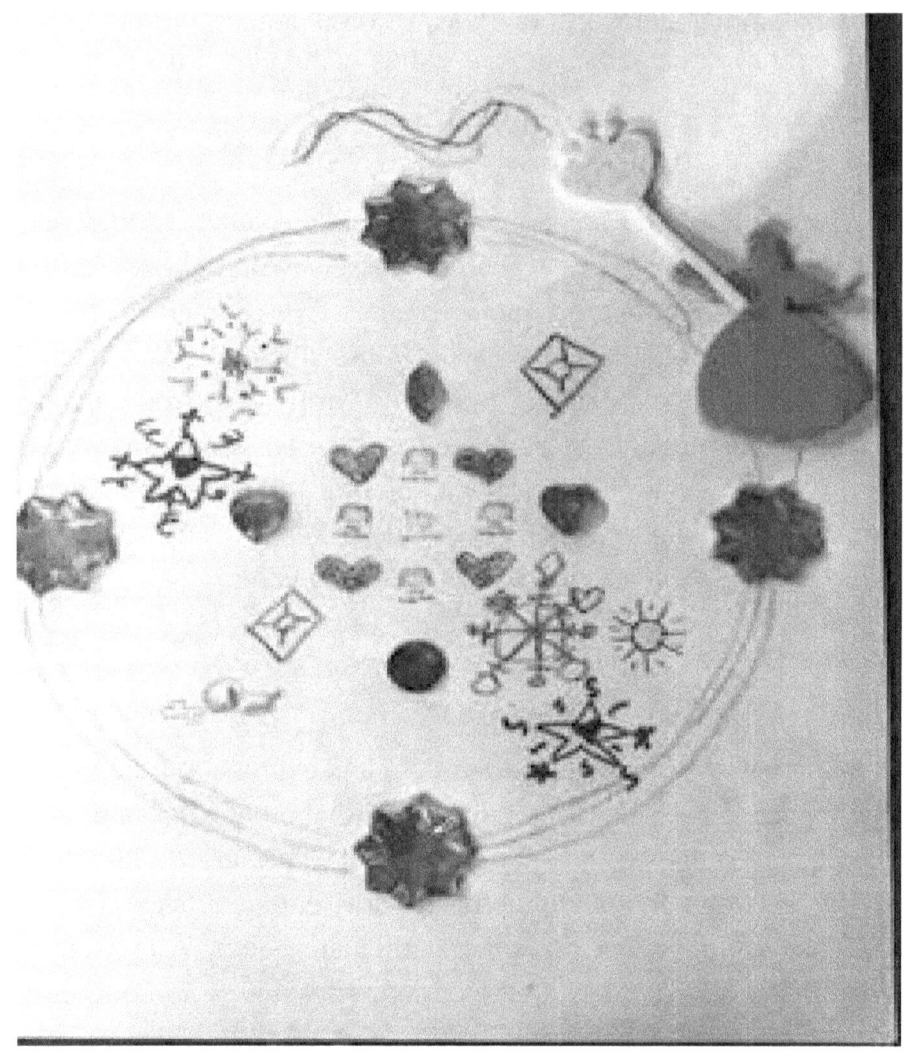

Mandala #26

Name: Feelings Cards Mandala

Level: All ages and groups

Materials: One deck of feelings playing cards (can be purchased online at many therapy sites.)

Procedure:
Follow Step #1. Explain how mandalas have most always been a circular shape since it can be very relaxing and feel safe creating artwork within a circle. Explain how you would like the client to think about the various feelings they have noticed within the past week/two weeks/month, or since the last visit. As I go through the cards and say each one out loud, I ask him/her to say "Yes", or "that one" if I name one that he/she has been experiencing. I do remind them before starting that it is quite normal to experience many feelings throughout a span of time. Once all feelings have been chosen by the client I invite him/her to place in the center of our space the feeling he/she has most been experiencing. When that is complete, I then advise to pick some more feelings that have been felt and place around the center card. If there are more feelings that have been chosen, I invite the client to continue the circular theme, placing the lesser intense feelings towards the outer ring of the mandala. I remind the client that we do not have to have a specific number of feelings, and are in control of how many feelings to place in the rings around the center card.

Discussion:
This particular intervention allows for processing throughout the entire creation phase. The therapist is an active participant, explaining the meaning of some feelings words, processing where to put the cards in terms of the intensity felt, and discussing what has been happening in the clients' lives to have prompted the cards chosen. This is a great way for clients to think about then express how they have been doing outside of therapy in a way other than using art. This is also a mandala creation that will need to be taken apart, so therapists should be aware of waiting until the client leaves, taking a picture, and then dismantling the mandala.

Feelings Cards Mandala

(Created by 6 year old client having difficulty in school with behavior and work completion. Titled "I Don't Like School")

Mandala #27

Name: Shield Mandala

Level: Ages six and up

Materials: Mandala ring templates in a variety of colors (cut out as a ring, with a hollow center. This is where the contact paper will go), pencil, crayons, markers, colored pencils, narrow paper strip (for shield handle), contact paper (have one sheet of contact paper, sticky side up, attached to the bottom of the mandala template)

Procedure:
Follow Step #1. Explain how shields have also been used for centuries, not only for protection but to identify a family clan or group. Tell the client that today a personal shield will be made to help identify who the client is. Give the client a minute or two to think about ways he/she is identified (examples include name, physical features, qualities, etc.) Discuss the client's personal qualities aloud and then have the client think of symbols that represent these identifications. Using construction paper, have the client draw and then cut out each symbol and place inside the mandala template on the sticky part of the contact paper. When all symbols are created and on the mandala, take another sheet of contact paper to place on the top of the mandala (Creating a top and bottom covering for the shield. Have the client cut any excess contact paper, and then tape a narrow paper strip to each side of the mandala to create the shield handle.

Discussion:
This intervention will allow some processing when initially discussing identifciations and personal qualities, but the therapist should take care to allow the creation process to be as quiet as possible. Clients may need some additional help applying the symbols to the contact paper, but most seem to accomplish this well. It helps to have the mandala templates pre-cut with the contact paper fastened to the bottom of the template, but this may not be possible if you are unaware of the color the client would choose. Therapists could make sure they have one of these templates prepared in a variety of colors and then quickly place the contact paper on the bottom of whichever template the client chooses.

Discussion questions remain the same with perhaps the following additions:
- How does _____ (particular symbol) represent _____ (particular quality)?
- Is there a way that your particular qualities keep you safe? How?

- Are there any qualities that are detrimental rather than helpful? How?

Shield Mandala

(Created by a 9 year old client, using construction paper and contact paper, titled "Power Shield")

Mandala #28

Name: Stained Glass Mandala

Level: All ages and groups

Materials: White mandala template (cut out as a ring exactly as described in intervention #27), tissue paper, large sequins, contact paper, hole puncher, ribbon or yarn

Procedure:
Follow Step #1. Discuss that many churches and sometimes temples have stained glass designs that resemble mandalas, showing the beauty of the art and the expression of the artist. Explain to the client that today he/she will be creating a stained glass mandala of his/her own to take home and place in a window of his/her choosing. Have the white mandala ring template pre-cut so the middle is hollow, and have a piece of contact paper, sticky side up, underneath the template. Invite the client to use various colors of tissue paper, and to tear the pieces into whatever shapes/styles of his/her choosing. Typically a child's handful of tissue paper scraps is more than enough. When pieces are complete, allow the client to place inside of the mandala template on the sticky side of the contact paper. Client can also embellish with large sequins, offered in a small dish. When finished, place a second sheet of contact paper, sticky side down, on top of the mandala template and smooth. Allow the client to cut any left-over edges of contact paper. Have client, or help them if younger, punch a hole in the top of the mandala and thread the ribbon through to hang up at home.

Discussion:
This is one of the most popular mandala creations for a variety of reasons. For one, clients get to tear and rip tissue paper, which can feel quite relaxing and freeing. They don't have to be concerned about their designs being perfect or just to their specifications. They are able to carefully place the tissue shapes on the contact paper, and almost immediately see the beautiful results. They can also take this mandala home more as an art piece without having to explain the meaning to others. I especially like this intervention for my younger, or more dysregulated clients since the tearing seems to relax them greatly.

Stained Glass Mandala

(Created by a twelve year old client, titled "Beautiful")

Mandala #29

Name: Coffee Filter Mandala

Level: All ages and groups

Materials: Coffee filter, washable markers, small spray bottle of water, cardboard, table cloth or other protective covering, black and white construction paper, paper towels for cleaning

Procedure:
Follow Step #1. Explain how often what is originally intended to be created is not the end result. This is what can be the "beautiful unknowing" of art. Place the coffee filter on top of a white piece of paper, on top of a piece of heavy cardboard paper, and have a plastic table cloth or drop cloth/canvas underneath for extra absorption. Hand the client washable markers and instruct him/her to create any type of design on the coffee filter. You may wish to remind the client that coffee filters are thin and can tear easily, so color lightly. Another reminder is that this picture will change quite a bit so it may be better to stick with designs and shapes rather than an actual picture. Remain quiet while the client creates his/her design. When finished, hand the client the spray bottle and instruct to spray the coffee filter however little or much he/she desires. Caution them that he/she can always add water spray, but can not take away, so a little initially may be best. Watch with the client as the art work changes into an abstract, colorful masterpiece! The paper underneath the coffee filter offers a second piece of art to keep or share. When dry, mount the coffee filter mandala onto a piece of black paper to easily display.

Discussion:
I find it so enjoyable to watch the awe in children's eyes as something created "morphs" into something else. There is great joy when the art work turns into an abstract painting! Typically children continue to spray water due to the joy they feel when watching the colors expand and blend into each other. I try to have many paper towels handy to help keep the water contained to the filter. This project also dries very quickly so can be taken home the same day. In groups, I have allowed each member to give one spray at a time so they can slowly see how all of their sprays have made a difference in the final product.

Additional questions which may be processed are:
- **How did you notice your masterpiece changing while you were spraying it?**

- In what ways can you change to help you feel better/more relaxed/balanced?
- Water is often associated with "fresh starts", cleansing, fluidity. Are there areas in your life you would like to "spray away and start clean"? How could you make that happen?

Coffee Filter Mandala

(Created by a six year old client, untitled)

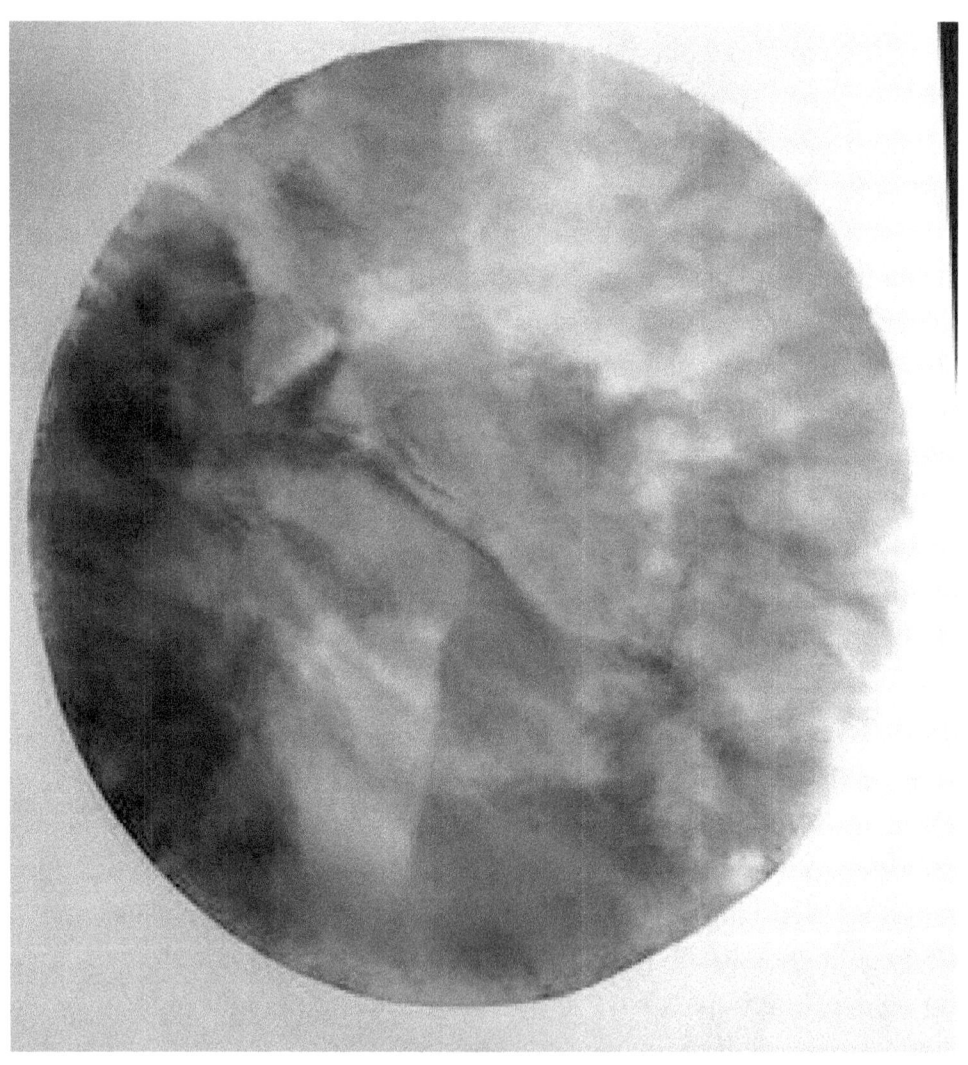

Mandala #30

Name: Foil Mandala

Level: All ages and groups (under age six will need help)

Materials: Cardboard mandala template, glue, thick yarn, foil, permanent markers, scissors

Procedure:
Follow Step #1. Explain how three-dimensional mandalas could be created by using rocks, powders, and other natural elements. Discuss how today we will create a three-dimensional/textured mandala with shiny foil. Hand the client the cardboard mandala template and the glue, and instruct to make any type of glue design he/she wishes. When finished, cut a long piece of yarn and have the client place the yarn on top of the glue creation, pressing down firmly so the yarn will hold. Some clients will find it easier to use several, shorter pieces of yarn rather than one piece of yarn. Allow ten to fifteen minutes for the yarn to adhere to the glue. Give the client a large sheet of foil and instruct him/her to wrap the mandala carefully with the foil. Remind the client that the back of the mandala will not be part of the artwork, so it is o.k. for the foil to look messy in the back. When the mandala is wrapped have the client smooth and press gently on the foil so the raised areas will be noticed (where the yarn was placed). Once completed to the client's liking, allow him/her to use permanent markers carefully to design the mandala.

Discussion:
This mandala has multi-sensory components that are well liked by many clients. Visually, the clients enjoy the shiny foil, and how the colors added look jewel-toned. They also enjoy the touch component of placing the yarn on the glue, wrapping the mandala, and pressing on the foil and feeling the yarn underneath. This mandala is often taken home and used as a calming device to help regulate clients.

Foil Mandala

(Created by a 4 year old client titled "Bear")

Mandala #31

Name: Secret Mandala

Level: Ages six and up

Materials: Two paper mandala templates with a door-type design cut out of one of them, pencil, crayons, markers, colored pencils, glue stick, tape

Procedure:
The therapist may choose to already have the templates created if working with younger clients, or on time constraints. If not, hand the client the first paper template and explain how a door should be cut out of it. Remind the client that the door should only have three cut marks so it can fold open and close. Allow the client to create the door to be any size, anywhere on the mandala. When finished, have the client glue around the edge of the second template with a glue stick, then place the "door mandala" on top. Explain how mandalas have been created for centuries to help people realize their hopes and dreams. Often times, we keep these dreams secret out of fear. We may fear failure, rejection, negativity, etc., and therefore keep our dreams secret. Have the client spend a few minutes thinking about one of his/her dreams, to be drawn on the bottom mandala to be hidden by the "door". Clients can use words, pictures, or symbols, and create with a pencil or with color. When completed explain how the client gets to choose how deeply he/she wishes to keep this dream secret. If complete secret is desired, a glue stick will be used to "close and seal the door". If secret for now is the answer, a piece of tape will be used, if ready to share, the door will not be fastened. Have the client then design the rest of the mandala using whatever shapes/images/designs he/she chooses.

Discussion:
I created this mandala intervention as an affirmation to my clients. I wanted them to know the importance of dreams, and how to set reasonable goals to achieve these dreams. I also wanted my clients to know that they are allowed to choose when to share their dreams and when to keep them to themselves. The modification of using tape to close the door gives them the additional freedom of saying "Not yet, but soon". My clients seem to love the sense of power that comes with this intervention. They are able to see that their dreams are valuable, worthy, and theirs to keep in their heart, or to share when ready.
An additional discussion question may be:

- **In what ways can you take small steps towards achieving your dreams right now?**

Mandala #32

Name: Snowflake Mandala

Level: Ages four and up as well as groups

Materials: Mandala template using thin paper or coffee filter, scissors, pastels

Procedure:
Follow Step #1. Check to see if the client has ever created a snowflake out of paper. Hand the client the mandala template and explain that he/she will be creating a snowflake mandala. Have the client fold the circle in half, fourths, or as many times as he/she chooses and then cut designs on the edges and tip of the paper. Often times, drawing the design first and then cutting is ideal. When cutting is complete, open the mandala to see the design. Have the client use oil pastels when coloring the snowflake mandala so as not to tear the artwork.

Discussion:
Paper snowflakes are fun, easy ways for children to create masterpieces of beauty. Snowflake mandalas have the additional element of color to further enhance the beauty of the cut-out. These mandalas are often glued onto a colorful piece of construction paper to visually see the cut-out design. Some clients choose to leave their mandala white, or do not choose to glue theirs to construction paper which is perfectly acceptable. Many teens especially love this intervention since it reminds them of their younger years.

An additional discussion may be:

- **No two snowflakes are alike. What qualities make you unique, like a snowflake?**

Mandala #33

Name: Medicine Wheel Mandala

Level: Ages four and up as well as groups

Materials: Medicine wheel template (on next page), red, white, yellow and black construction paper, pencil, crayons, markers, colored pencils, pastels

Procedure:
Explain how mandalas were created in Native American culture to aid in healing, exploration and harmony with all. One well-known Native American mandala is the Medicine Wheel mandala. This was seen as the *wheel of life* that all of us must walk. We are all protected by the four directions and aspects of the medicine wheel, both internally and externally. Describe the four colors of the medicine wheel and what each color represents (Can be found on the template on the following page). Hand the client the yellow quadrant and explain that he/she is to use words, symbols, and pictures to fill this quadrant with the theme of "birth". Next hand the client the red quadrant, and this theme is "childhood". The black quadrant will be "adulthood", and the white quadrant will be "old age". The client may choose to use this intervention as his/her own "Past, Present, Future" work of art, or use symbols and pictures that generally represent this theme to him/her. Remind the client of your silence during the creation and to indicate completion by telling you or ringing the gong. Begin by ringing the gong.

Discussion:
There tends to be a great deal of processing that occurs with this intervention! So much so that I often complete the "birth" and "childhood" quadrants and processing in one session, then the "adulthood" and "old age" quadrants and processing at the next session. This intervention creates a great deal of exploration, harmony and insight with clients of all ages. I have not conducted this intervention with adults, but I believe it would be meaningful with them as well.

Medicine Wheel Template

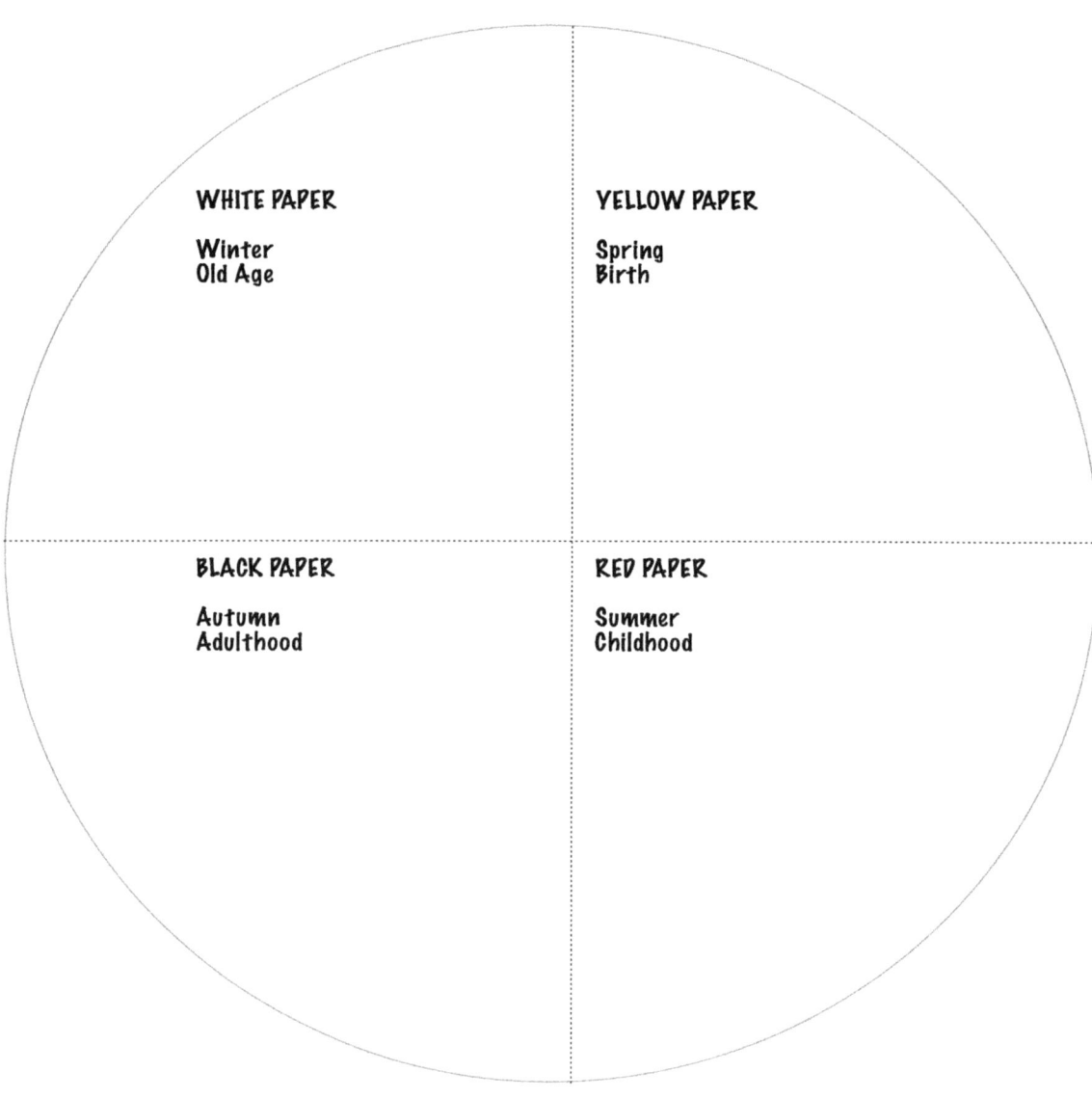

Mandala #34

Name: Glitter Mandala

Level: All ages and groups

Materials: Mandala template, glitter in assorted colors, colored pencils, glue, tablecloth or canvas to reduce mess

Procedure:
Discuss with the client how mandalas have been created for centuries to bring joy and relaxation to both the creators and the viewers. Hand the mandala to the client and explain how today's mandala will only be created using glitter. The client is to create shapes and designs out of glue and then shake glitter onto them. I first have the client take colored pencils of his/her choice and lightly draw ideas onto the template. This allows the client to know colors ahead of time so the glitter can be used one color at a time (preventing glitter mixing when putting the excess back into the tube). The therapist will remain quiet as much as possible during the creation, although most clients may need help with placing excess glitter back into the tube.

Discussion:
I was recently at a workshop where the participants were a mix of therapists and educators. The topic of glitter came up, and I discovered the vast majority of them no longer allow glitter in the therapy/classroom. I instantly realized this is why glitter may be such a hit in my playroom! I believe that mess should not be a consideration as to why an intervention isn't used. For particularly messy interventions, intentionally plan for a bit more time after the session for clean up. Glitter mandalas turn out to be beautiful, and allow clients a different medium for creating works of art. They should not be avoided, but enjoyed.

Glitter Mandala

(Created by a five year old client, titled "Sparkly")

Mandala #35

Name: Me in My Mandala

Level: All ages

Materials: Mandala template, paper, mirror, glue stick, pencil, crayons, markers and colored pencils

Procedure:
Follow Step #1. The client begins today's mandala by first drawing a self-portrait. Hand the client a small piece of paper (I use 1/4 of a white piece of construction paper) and a pencil and have him/her draw a self portrait. Remind client that these can be realistic or abstract. Provide a mirror if needed. Remain quiet while the client is creating. When completed have the client cut out this self portrait and glue it onto the center of the mandala template. The client should then fill in the rest of the mandala using whatever designs/words/shapes/pictures of his/her choosing. Remind the client of your silence during the creation and to indicate completion by telling you or ringing the gong. Begin by ringing the gong.

Discussion:
This tends to be an insightful mandala intervention for all ages. It is interesting to see what designs are chosen after the self-portrait is in place as the bindu. Clients should spend a minute or two really contemplating the finished product before processing the mandala.

Additional discussion questions may include:
- **What do you notice about your self portrait? Any feelings about the self portrait?**
- **Tell me how you chose the designs around the self portrait (color, shape, etc). How did your choices correspond with the notion that it was "you in the mandala"?**

Me in My Mandala

(Created by sixteen year old client, titled "Self Portrait")

Mandala #36

Name: Shape Mandala

Level: All ages and groups

Materials: Mandala template, pencil, crayons, markers and colored pencils

Procedure:
Follow Step #1. Discuss how shapes are one of the first things we learn to draw as children, and how we continue to use them often to help in our masterpieces. Shapes can also be found in nature, and we tend to use them to make special patterns and designs. If needed, review various shapes to help the client in his/her masterpiece. Hand the client the mandala template and invite him/her to fill it with whatever shapes are appealing. The bindu is the very center of the mandala, and may be filled with the most important or special shape to the client. The client may choose to use one, or many shapes, and can design with pencil only or with color. Let him/her know that you will be remaining quiet during the creation, and to please let you know when finished. He/she can also indicate completion by ringing the gong. Begin by ringing the gong.

Discussion:
As discussed in Chapter 4, shapes can be revealing to therapists, and creating them might reveal any particular feelings clients may be experiencing. I have also noticed that this intervention can be less threatening to those clients who don't feel particularly creative. Creating a mandala out of shapes which clients have drawn for years seems to take any undue pressure off of them that they may be feeling. I have seen many beautiful mandalas created out of one, or various shapes and have gained a lot of insight when processing these with clients. One particular client used all hearts in her mandala, and then drew jagged lines carefully through each one. This told me more about her recent breakup than any words could.

Mandala #37

Name: Element Mandala

Level: Ages six and up

Materials: Pictures of the four elements (fire, wind, water, earth), mandala template, pencil, crayons, markers, colored pencils

Procedure:
Follow Step #1. Have pictures of the four elements and explain how each can represent something within people:

Fire: Courage and strength
Water: Healing and dreams
Air: Intelligence and learning
Earth: Stability and order

Hand the client the mandala template and explain how this mandala will be completed with the theme of the elements. The client is able to choose one, two, three, or all of the elements and create symbols, pictures, shapes and/or words to express how the elements are represented within him/her. The client is welcome to divide the mandala into equal parts, or have all of the elements represented throughout the mandala. Explain that there is no right or wrong way to complete this activity. Let him/her know that you will be remaining quiet during the creation, and to please let you know when finished. He/she can also indicate completion by ringing the gong. Begin by ringing the gong.

Discussion:
This mandala intervention helps clients look within themselves and discover the inner qualities they have. I often give clients time to think about how these elements correspond with who they are and with how they relate to the world. Clients are very creative and intuitive in their masterpieces.

An additional question during processing may be:
- What qualities of the _____ element do you currently have? What qualities would you like to develop?

Mandala #38

Name: Two Sides of Me Mandala

Level: Ages six and up as well as groups

Materials: Mandala template, pencil, crayons, markers, colored pencils, additional craft materials if needed

Procedure:
Follow Step #1. Discuss and process how we often feel like there are two sides to us. Process examples of this concept. (Examples may include: my talkative vs. my shy side, my serious vs. my silly side, my confident vs. my unsure side, etc.) Hand the client the mandala template and explain how this piece of art will show one example of the two sides of him/her. Remind the client that he/she can choose which symbols, words, shapes or pictures to use; there is no right or wrong way of completing this. Remind the client of your silence during the creation and to indicate completion by telling you or ringing the gong. Begin by ringing the gong.

Discussion:
Although there is a great deal of processing before this mandala creation, I am careful to remain quiet while clients are creating their masterpieces. This intervention is personal and introspective and I want to make sure they have the quiet they need to process their feelings while creating.

Processing questions have proven to be very powerful and may include:
- Is one area stronger than the other? Would you like for that to be different?
- Which side does your family see more? Your friends? Your teacher? New people?

Two Sides of Me Mandala

(Created by a nine year old client. He stated the light sabers used by one good, one evil Star Wars character represents the good and bad in him)

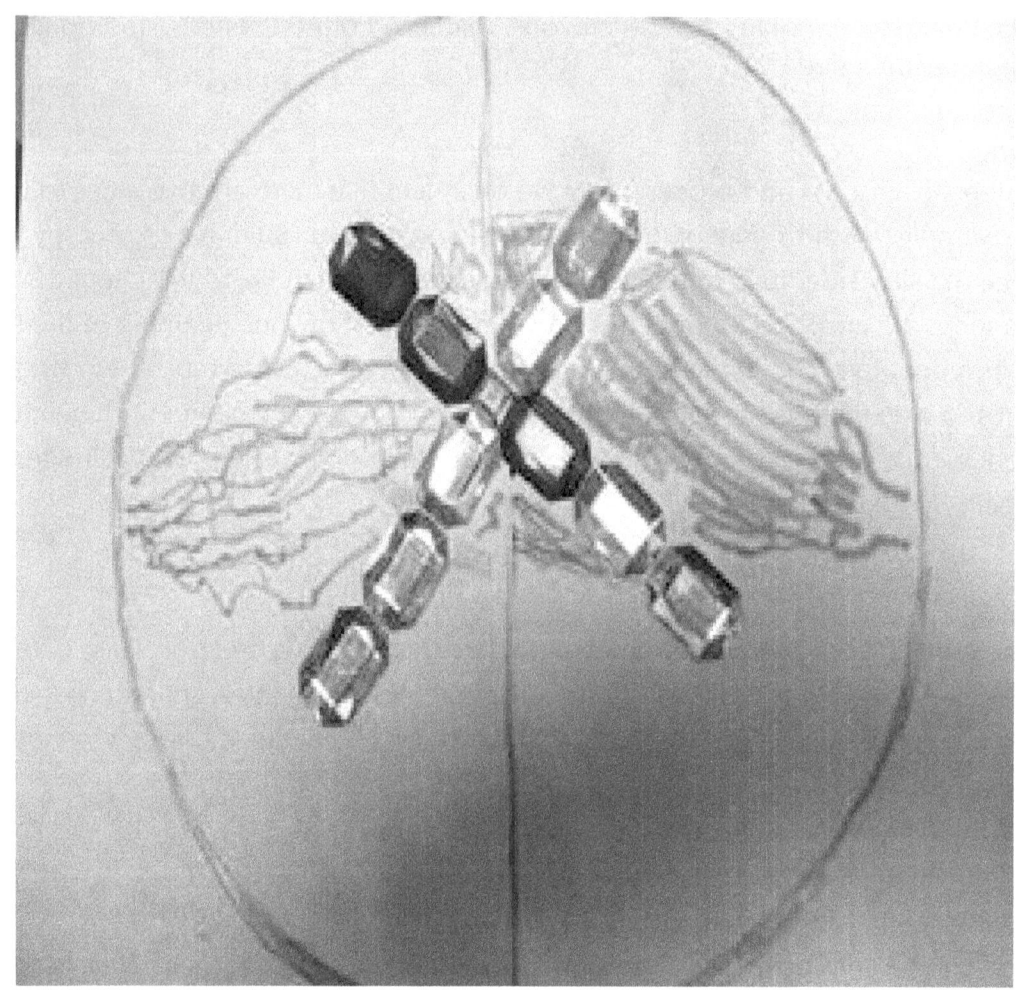

Mandala #39

Name: Sensory Mandala

Level: Ages six and up as well as groups

Materials: Foam mandala template (found in craft stores), classical music, scented markers, drop cloth or canvas, Optional: blindfold or bandana

Procedure:
Follow Step #1. Discuss how often times we feel calmer when we focus on senses other than vision. Give examples of scents, sounds, and textures that help us relax. Hand the client the foam mandala template and explain how today's artwork will focus on our other sessions excluding vision. Allow the client to choose three markers to use for this creation (so as not to overwhelm), and have him/her smell each one to recognize each scent. Once the markers are selected explain to the client that he/she will fill in the mandala with any shapes, colors or pictures he/she chooses. The challenge will be to create the mandala without looking at it. He/she can feel the mandala to know where it is located, smell the markers to know which color is being used, and listen to quiet music to help relax. Explain how the focus is not on perfection, but on using other senses to create art masterpieces. Be sure to place the drop cloth or canvas on the workspace, in case the client draws outside of the mandala. Remind the client of your silence during the creation and to indicate completion by telling you or ringing the gong. Turn on the music and begin by ringing the gong.

Discussion:
This intervention often does not stay quiet, since clients typically are vocal about the difficulty of not looking at their mandalas. Of course, if they are becoming frustrated they can peek down for guidance, but most enjoy the challenge of focusing on their other senses. When complete, I allow clients to change any piece of it they want (using their eyes this time), but will say that most choose to keep it as it is.

Additional discussion questions may be:
- Describe how it was focusing on your other senses to create this masterpiece.
- How can you use your other senses when feeling stressed?

Sensory Mandala

(Created by a twelve year old client, titled "Love")

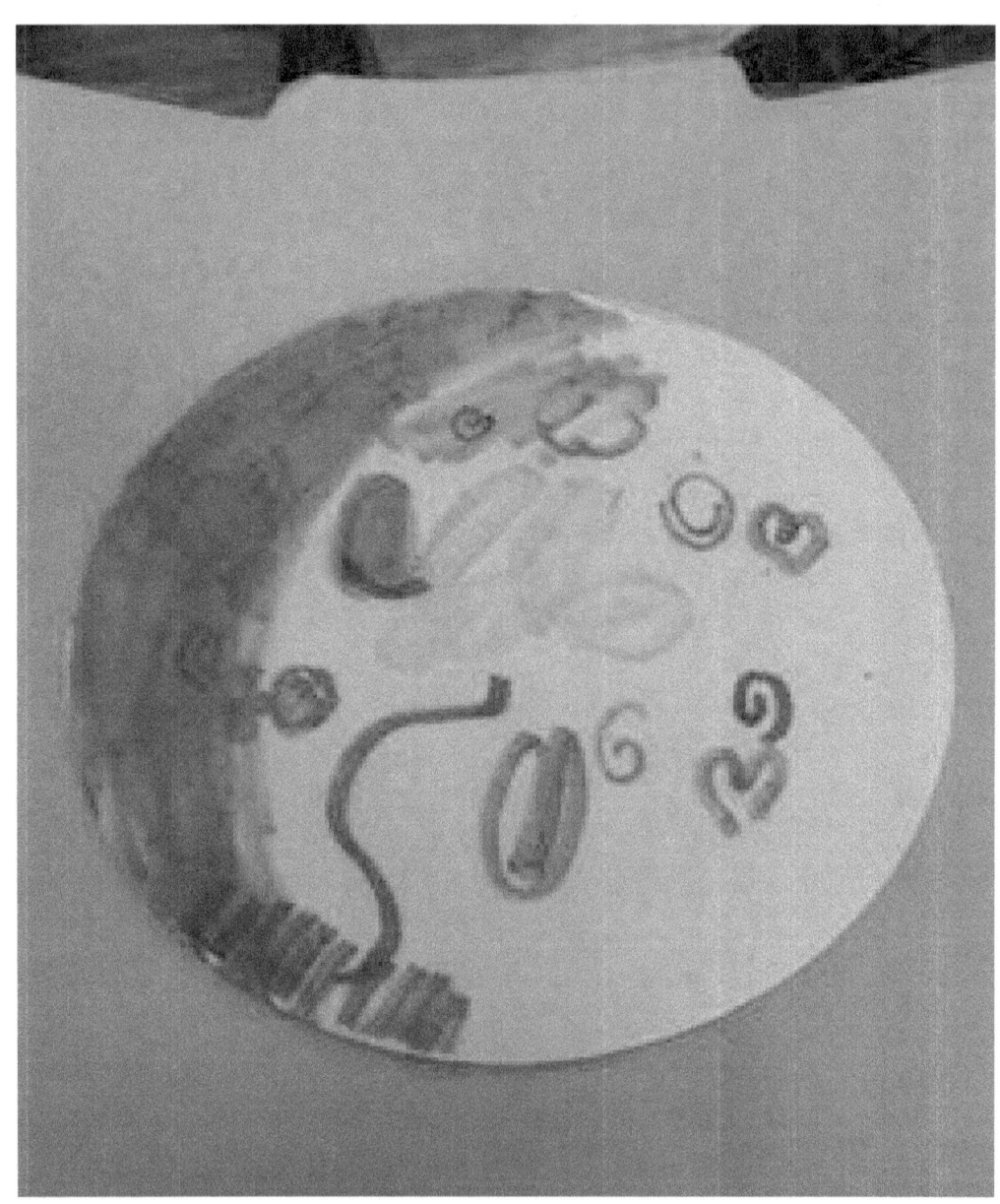

Mandala #40

Name: Timeline Mandala

Level: Ages six and up as well as groups

Materials: Paper plate, ruler, pencil, crayons, markers, colored pencils

Procedure:
Follow Step #1. Explain how looking back to past events can help us see into our present state, and how planning future goals can help us decide our current focus. Hand the client the mandala template and have him/her write numbers on it just like a clock (older clients can use the clock design, but count by 2's to reach more ages). The client may also wish to add lines so each number has a corresponding segment. When finished explain that the client can fill any segments he/she wishes with past/present/future highlights and events. The client can choose to fill in as many segments as he/she desires, and can use pictures, words, symbols to depict each moment. Remind the client of your silence during the creation and to indicate completion by telling you or ringing the gong. Begin by ringing the gong.

Discussion:
This is a fun and engaging way to build rapport with clients. It allows the therapist to learn more about the client's past, as well as future goals and dreams. I often remind clients that they can focus on any memory they choose, both happy and sad. This allows them an opportunity to open up about any traumas or disappointments they may have experienced.

Timeline Mandala

(Created by a nine year old client who used the timeline for past, present and future memories/ideas)

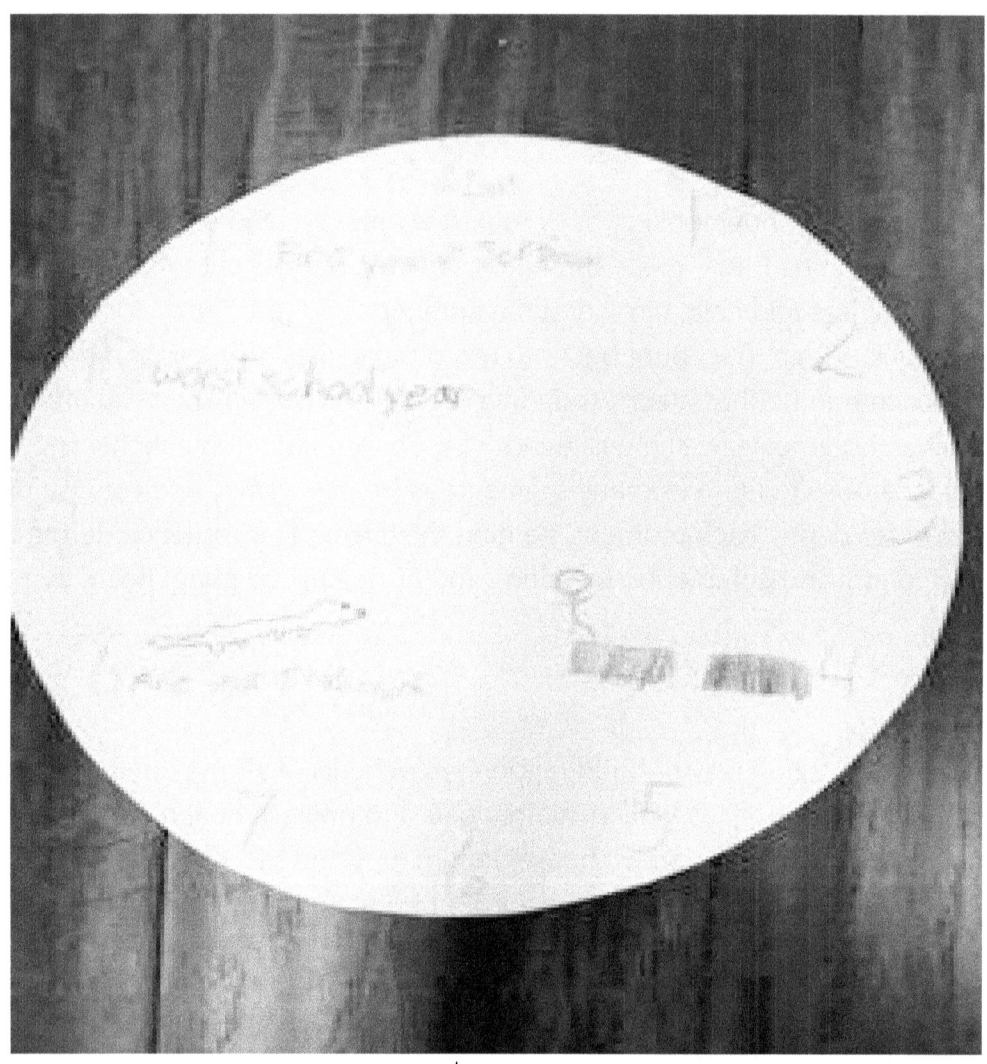

Mandala #41

Name: Light/Dark Mandala

Level: All ages as well as groups

Materials: One half circle of white construction paper, one half circle of black construction paper, tape, pastels, chalks, paint pens, gel pens

Procedure:
Follow Step #1. Discuss how different colors can evoke different feelings, as well as the concept of light vs. dark. Hand the client both the white and the black half of the mandala and have him/her first process the feelings and emotions felt when looking at both of the colors. Then explain that he/she will be able to fill in both halves of the mandala using whatever colors, shapes, words and symbols feel right to him/her. Let him/her know that you will be remaining quiet during the creation, and to please let you know when finished. He/she can also indicate completion by ringing the gong. Begin by ringing the gong. When finished, client can tape the halves together to have a complete mandala.

Discussion:
This mandala intervention is a great way to introduce clients to creating on both light and dark templates. Pastels, chalks, paint pens or gel pens are the perfect mediums to use on both the white and the black halves of the mandala since the color will appear more vivid. Provide a limited choice of these options so as not to overwhelm. Although many clients view the white half of the paper as the "happy/good" side and the black half of the paper the "mad/bad" side, this is not always the case, and can be explored.

Additional processing questions may include:
- Describe the feelings you experience when viewing the white half of the mandala vs. the black half of the mandala.
- What are some common opinions you have on the color white/black? Are these accurate? Can you think of exceptions?

Light/Dark Mandala
(Created by nine year old client. Used red since that is his favorite color and created symbols to represent light and dark)

Mandala #42

Name: Animal Mask Mandala

Level: All ages and groups

Materials: Round paper plate for mandala template, craft stick, glue, crayons, markers, colored pencils

Procedure:
Follow Step #1. Discuss how humans how long been interested in animals and have often associated certain qualities to specific animals. Process with the client examples of this (Examples include monkeys being silly, elephants never forgetting, sharks being fierce, etc.) Have the client think of an animal that most represents who he/she is. Once an animal is selected, hand the client the mandala template and allow him/her to draw this animal's face on the mandala using whatever medium of his/her choosing. Explain how any shapes, images, symbols or color can be chosen to represent this animal. Remind the client of your silence during the creation and to indicate completion by telling you or ringing the gong. Begin by ringing the gong.

Discussion
Most children and teens are drawn to animals and can easily relate to them. Having them pick a particular animal gives therapists great insight into the current feelings of self the client may have. Clients may choose to use this mandala as a mask, or keep it as an art masterpiece. Therapists should have scissors on hand in case clients wish to cut out the eyes if they want the mandala to be a mask.

It is important to remember that associations or symbolism with a particular animal may be quite different for therapist and client. Discussion is key! As an example, I love snakes, and I had a pet snake several years ago. If I were to draw a snake it would be to show the curious, intelligent nature I have noticed about these animals. A therapist would be mistaken to assume that this snake had a different meaning than this. Which leads to the very important discussion question:

- **Tell me about the qualities of the animal you chose. In what ways does this animal resemble you?**

Mandala #43

Name: Mud/Lotus Mandala

Level: Ages six and up as well as groups

Materials: Mud/Lotus template on following page, picture of lotus, crayons, markers, colored pencils

Procedure:
Follow Step #1. Ask the child if he/she has any information on the lotus flower. (Have a picture provided for reference; they are easily found online.) Explain, if the child did not know, that the roots of a lotus flower grow deep underneath the pond. The beginnings of the roots are found in the very muddy bottom of the pond; the roots then rise above the water which creates the beautiful lotus flower. If it wasn't for the yucky mud, the lotus would not be able to create such a beautiful flower. (Using Venerable Thich Nhat Hanh's words "No Mud, No Lotus") Discuss how this is a wonderful metaphor for our own lives. We may have lots of "yucky muddy" things occurring in our lives, but if we settle in, grow through the chaos, and then rise above the chaos we can become beautiful flowers of our own. Hand the client the mud/lotus template and have him/her think about the "yucky muddy" things in his/her life. The bottom part of the template below the line is where the client can create words, symbols or pictures to represent these difficult things. Have the client next think about ways he/she can rise above this chaos to become a beautiful flower. The top part of the template above the line is where the client can create words, symbols or pictures to represent these beautiful qualities. Remind the client of your silence during the creation and to indicate completion by telling you or ringing the gong. Begin by ringing the gong.

Discussion:
I created this intervention soon after learning about the beautiful lotus flower. I was struck by this metaphor and instantly thought of the "yucky" things in my life that actually helped make me who I am. I continue to think of this metaphor, using the mantra "No mud, no lotus" when things feel particularly rough. I have found that my clients are moved by this intervention.

Mud-Lotus Mandala Template

Mandala #44

Name: Food Mandala

Level: All ages and groups

Materials: Small plate or ramekin, various types of fresh fruit, plastic knife, vegetables and nuts, hand sanitizer

Procedure:
Follow Step #1. Explain how mandalas have been created out of various objects, and many times mandalas are taken apart afterwards to show how nothing lasts forever. Tell how today's mandala will be created out of food and taken apart so it can be eaten! Provide client with a small saucer or larger ramekin. Have on display various types of fruits, vegetables and nuts (make sure client has no food allergies ahead of time; this is a question on my intake form). Have precut fruit slices, and have a plastic knife handy in case the client wants to create different shapes. Explain to client that he/she will first pick a bindu out of any of the items to place directly in the middle of the saucer. He/she will then choose various items to make second and third rings around the bindu, in an effort to create a mandala within the saucer. Remind the client of your silence during the creation and to indicate completion by telling you or ringing the gong. Begin by ringing the gong. When finished, discuss in brief all of the parts of nature/people/etc. that made this food possible for the client and create a gratitude mantra.

Discussion:
I have noticed with my clients that "dismantling the mandala" is much easier when the mandala is able to be eaten! This intervention gives an additional therapeutic highlight of the sharing of food. In many cultures, food is viewed as a gift, and the sharing of food is a treasure. Some religions and cultures view the sharing of food as a sacrament, ritual, or rite; it is that special. I remember one particular client from a different country who would bring me a small gift of food at every session to show her appreciation. She explained this was part of her culture, and that the sharing of food was seen as sacred. This intervention provides the additional sensory components of smell, touch, and eventually taste, while also having the child practice patience in not being able to eat right away. Below is the mantra that my clients and I typically say; feel free to create your own.

"Food is a gift, given to us by many. Thank you to all"

Food Mandala
(Created using strawberries, halo oranges, mini carrots and pistachios)

Mandala #45

Name: Lyric Mandala

Level: Ages eight and up as well as groups

Materials: Mandala template, computer to look up song lyrics, pencil, crayons, markers, colored pencils

Procedure:
Follow Step #1. Discuss how music is a deep component in many people's lives and can be moving and personal. Have the client think of a particular song that seems to speak to him/her, and then use the internet to look up the chosen song. Look over the lyrics together, and process possible meanings of the song. Hand the client the mandala template and invite him/her to create a masterpiece by using particular lyrics to the song chosen, as well as any other shapes, pictures and symbols desired. It is up to the client to decide whether to use specific parts of the song, or the song in its entirety. Remind the client of your silence during the creation and to indicate completion by telling you or ringing the gong. Begin by ringing the gong.

Discussion:
This mandala intervention seems to be particularly effective with teen clients. Songs seem to be the most meaningful at this developmental stage, and their favorite songs often have something to do with how they are feeling at the moment. I have learned a lot about my clients through this activity. A note here, I personally do not limit what song they choose, meaning I am willing to accept if the song has profanity, crude language, violence, or other perceived "negatives". This will be processed at the appropriate time. It is understandable, though for some therapists to not feel this way, and a boundary may be set over what type of song is chosen. I often allow them to listen to the song while they are creating their mandalas which adds an additional component to the creation.

Additional questions that may be asked include:
- Which part(s) of the lyrics specifically speak to you?
- Do you believe these lyrics resonate with something you are currently experiencing? If so, in what way?

Mandala #46

Name: Dream Catcher Mandala

Level: Ages six and up as well as groups

Materials: Small paper plate, yarn, scissors, hole punch, pencil or marker, tape

Procedure:
Follow Step #1. Explain how one Native American tribe had the mothers and grandmothers create dream catchers for children to help catch any bad dreams during the night so the children would have only good dreams. Hand the child a paper plate and a hole punch. Process with the child any supportive and nurturing people in his/her life, and for each person listed, have the child punch a hole in the outer edge of the plate, creating a ring of holes around the circumference of the paper plate. The client or therapist next writes each supportive person's name on the back of the paper plate underneath each hole. When finished, the counselor asks the client to start with one of the people and explain how he/she shows support to the client. The client will then thread the yarn through the specific person's hole then tape the end of the yarn to the back of the plate. The client will continue to express how each person shows support, while threading the yarn through each person's hole. If the client wants a more intricate yarn design he or she may continue to describe more ways that each person shows support. When finished, the client can turn over the paper plate and observe the dream catcher design.

Discussion:
It can be very comforting for clients to process the love and support they have in their lives, be it relatives, neighbors, friends, or school personnel. Often times clients may feel hopeless or alone, and this intervention is a reminder that they are not. We will often tape yarn onto the finished mandala so the clients can hang it around their own bedposts as a dream catcher. It helps many children sleep better when they remember the love that is felt for them.

Additional discussion questions may include:
- What does this teach us about giving and getting love and support from others?
- In what ways can you show support to those listed on your dream catcher?

Dream Catcher Mandala

(Created by ten year old client. On the back he listed the names of people he can count on in his life)

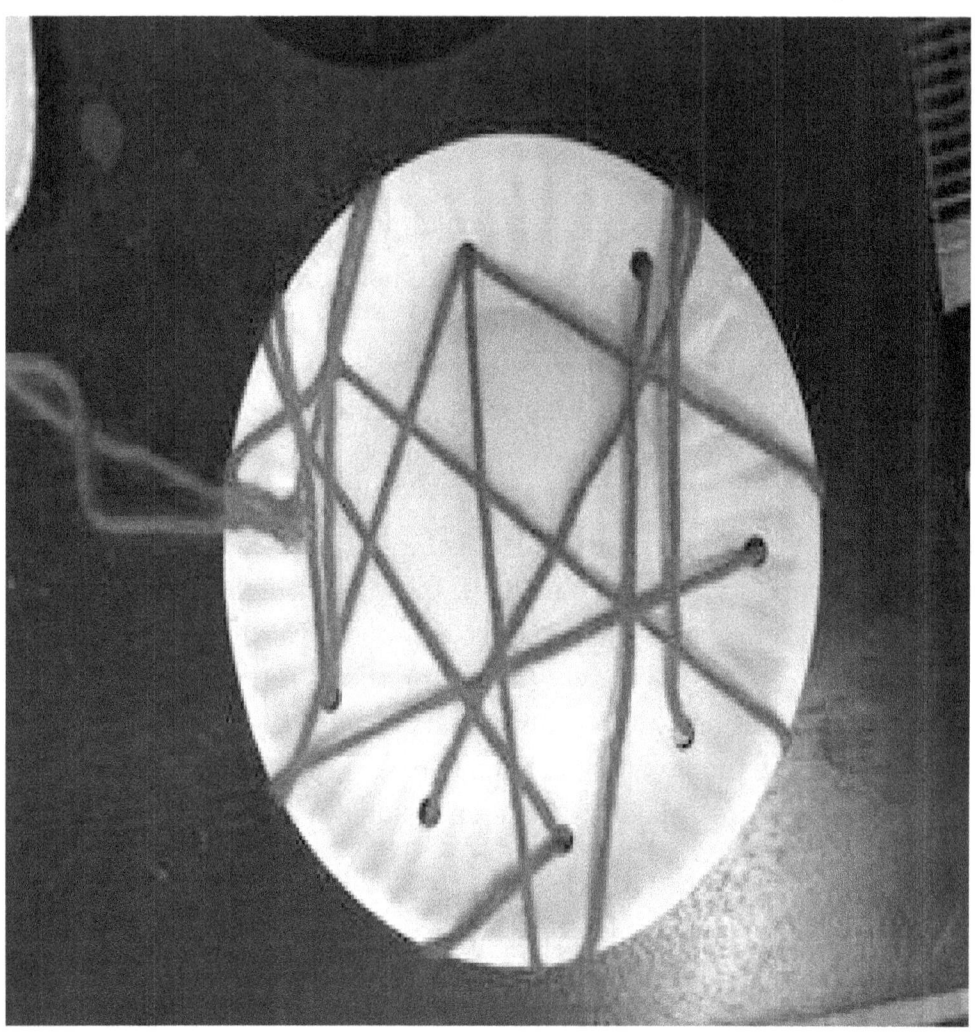

Mandala #47

Name: Collage Mandala

Level: Ages four and up as well as groups

Materials: Mandala template, magazines (travel and food are the best), scissors, glue stick

Procedure:
Follow Step #1. Discuss how many mandalas were created out of materials such as stones, leaves and jewels. Explain how a collage mandala is made out of magazine pages, using part of the page, or even one object on the page to fill the mandala with designs. The mandala can be filled completely, or only partially using whatever pictures and designs of the client's choosing. It may be recommended to first cut out specific pictures, place on the mandala, and then glue when the desired design is achieved. A younger client may enjoy tearing the pictures instead of using a scissors. Remind the client of your silence during the creation and to indicate completion by telling you or ringing the gong. Begin by ringing the gong.

Discussion:
This is yet another mandala intervention that is often popular with clients who do not necessarily enjoy coloring. Travel and food magazines are wonderful resources since the pictures are typically very bright and colorful. Travel magazines especially seem to tap into clients future dreams and wishes, and can be very beneficial. When I initially created this intervention I assumed that clients would fill the page with overlapping pictures, but am often surprised at the artistic designs they create while leaving blank space within the mandala. I continue to be amazed at the creativity of children!

Collage Mandala

(Created by ten year old client, who chose pictures of things she loved and cut them into a circle and petal shapes. Titled "Flower")

Mandala #48

Name: Personal Symbol Mandala

Level: Ages four and up as well as groups

Materials: Mandala template, examples of symbols ("S" from Superman for example), pencil, crayons, markers, colored pencils

Procedure:
Follow Step #1. Discuss how various symbols representative of a culture's traditions are often found in ancient mandalas. There are many modern day personal symbols given to super heroes, groups and teams. Have the client take several moments to think about an object or design that may be an inspirational symbol for him/her. This can be a recognizable symbol, or the client can create a symbol. The client may want to spend some time doodling to discover an appropriate symbol that feels just right. When ready, hand the client the mandala template and invite him/her to create a mandala using the personal symbol as the subject. The mandala can be filled however the client chooses, either using the symbol once, or many times throughout the masterpiece. Remind the client of your silence during the creation and to indicate completion by telling you or ringing the gong. Begin by ringing the gong.

Discussion:
I was attending the International Play Therapy Conference in 2014 when I was first introduced to the idea of a personal symbol. As a foster mom to dogs, I created a personal symbol that represented the ability to love fully, then let go completely. I was moved while creating this symbol, and I still think of the design to guide me when saying goodbye to my foster dogs. I thought it only right to introduce this personal symbol concept to mandala creation. It can be a powerful tool that allows clients to see their own individual strengths and identity.

Additional discussion questions may include:
- What does your personal symbol tell someone about you?
- How can your personal symbol help you cope in times of sorrow or trouble?
- What feelings of power does your symbol evoke in you? (Examples: strength, steadiness, fluidity, deep breaths, one foot in front of the other, etc.)

Personal Symbol Mandala

(Created by eight year old client, titled "Strong")

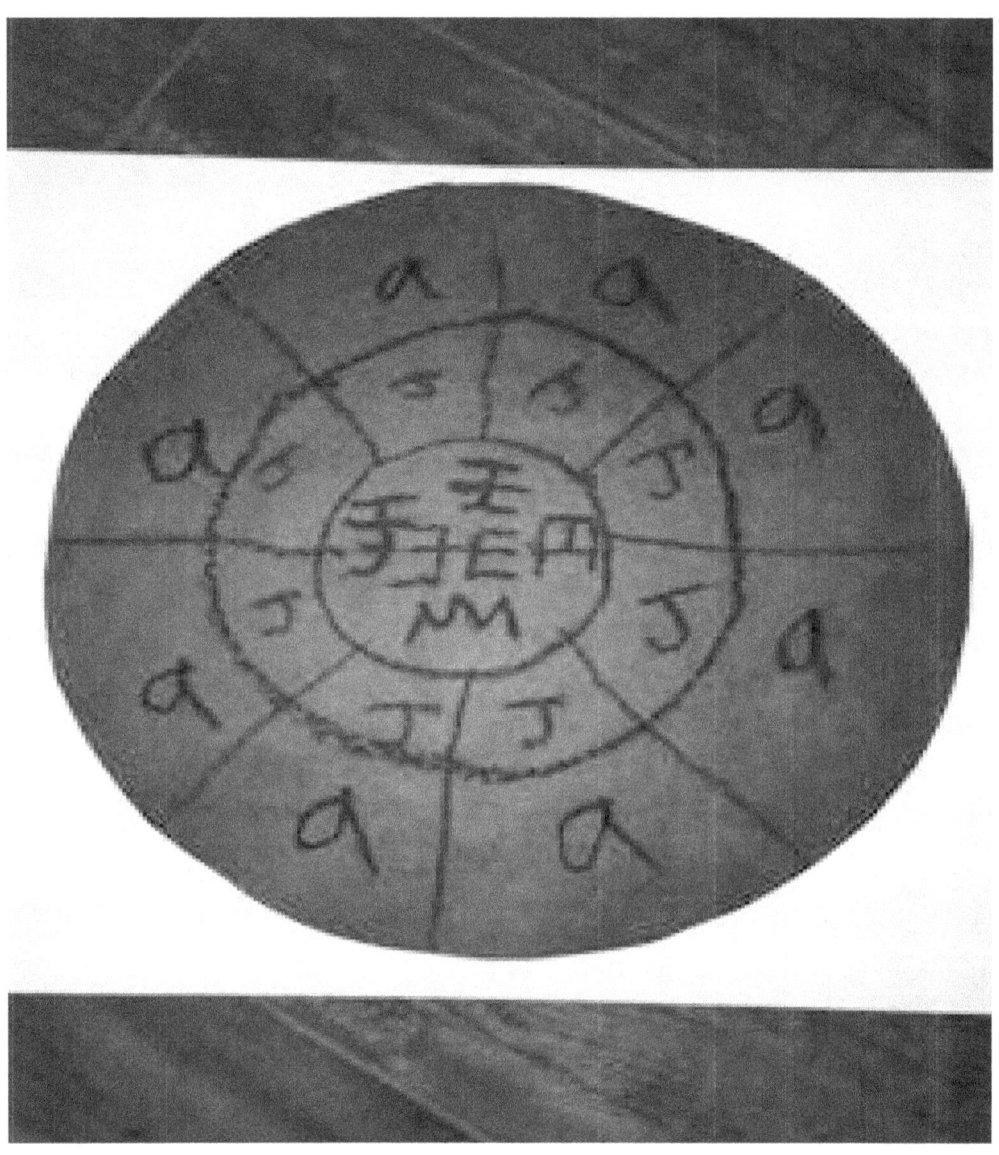

Mandala #49

Name: Sibling Mandala/Family Mandala

Level: Ages four and up, at least two siblings or family members

Materials: Same materials as Multi Media Mandala, mandala template cut in half/thirds/fourths depending on the number of siblings or family members. Optional: poster board

Procedure:
Follow Step #1. Discuss how Buddhist monks often work in groups of four to create large, detailed sand mandalas. Each monk focuses on his own design, yet the mandala comes together into one beautiful work of art. Hand each sibling a part of the mandala and explain how he/she can fill this piece with any designs, pictures or shapes of his/her choosing. Express to them the importance of creating what feeling is "right" to them (resonates with them), and to not worry about the finished product. Remind the participants of your silence during the creation and to each indicate completion by telling you or ringing the gong. Begin by ringing the gong. When all are finished, connect the mandala pieces to form one mandala.

Discussion:
This is a fun intervention to use with siblings, groups, or in family therapy. It is especially interesting to process the individual pieces of the mandala, and then the mandala as a whole. The individual results are quite striking, and the finished product turns out beautifully. Most siblings/families choose to tape the mandala together to bring home to display. Have construction paper or poster board on hand if families wish to display as a whole.

Processing questions remain the same with the exception of focusing on the pieces first and then the whole.

Sibling Mandala

(Created by twin, seven year old brothers, using markers, glitter glue and duct tape. Untitled)

Mandala #50

Name: All About Me Mandala

Level: Ages four and up as well as groups

Materials: Mandala template, pencil, crayons, markers, colored pencils

Procedure:
Follow Step #1. Hand the client the mandala template and instruct him/her to fill the mandala with anything he/she wishes to help me know more about who he/she is. Any shapes, pictures, words or symbols may be used, in whatever way feels right. Remind the client of your silence during the creation and to indicate completion by telling you or ringing the gong. Begin by ringing the gong.

Discussion:
Although this is the last mandala intervention in this book, it is often used as my first. This is a wonderful intervention to use at the first session with any client. It may also be used after several sessions when rapport has been established and more personal symbols may then be used. I have noticed firsthand how much more relaxed the clients seem to be while creating their mandala masterpieces as opposed to working on a traditional piece of paper. The circle design truly is special and sacred! I am impressed with the time and energy that goes into their personal mandalas, and I gain a great deal of insight during processing.

All About Me Mandala

(Created by a four year old client, titled "Me")

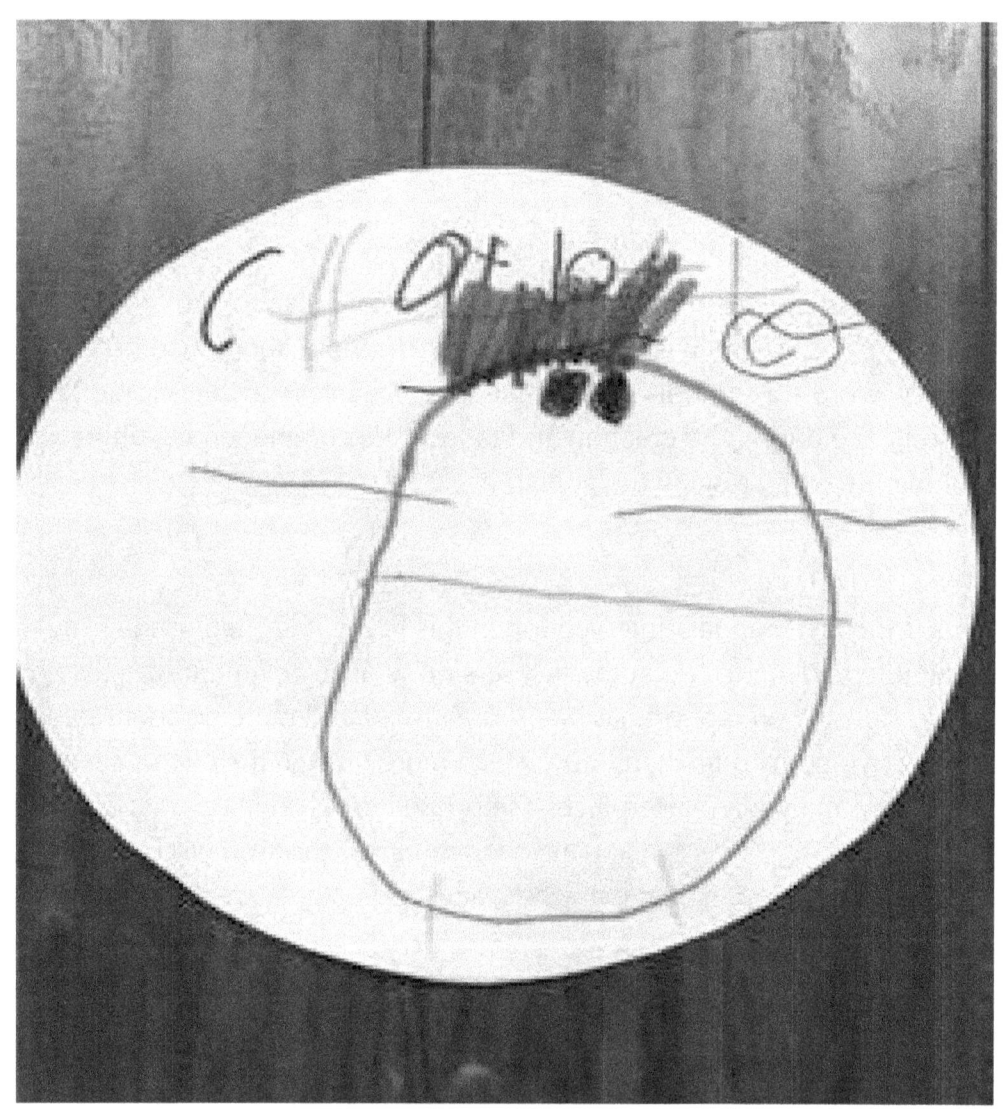

Chapter 9

Final Thoughts

"I found I could say things with color and shapes that I couldn't say any other way- things I had no words for."
-Georgia O'Keefe

What a gift it is to be a part of this all-important profession of therapy. We are both active and present members of the transformation of children! From the initial session, where mistrust and suffering are forefront, to the final session, where strength and independence is found, we are part of this beautiful process. I often think with humility of the giant step it must take for those seeking the help of the therapist, and am in awe of the strength that is needed for such an endeavor. I am not so naive as to think that I, or any other therapist, is immune from needing this help. We therapists are indeed on the front line, dealing daily with the emotional, mental and psychological pain of others; it is imperative that our needs are met as well. Either through the help of a therapist, or our own individualized care plan, we must take care of ourselves.

This need for self-care is what prompted my endeavor of using mandala interventions with clients. I personally have found coloring mandalas so healing, so relaxing. I then began creating nature mandalas with children's groups and church members who would come to our Buddhist temple to visit. I saw the great joy and peace that filled the groups when creating these works of art. I began using mandala interventions when conducting Play Therapy workshops, and saw stressed out, overworked participants cry with release upon viewing their creations. It was only logical to take the step of bringing mandala interventions into the therapy room.

I have learned from these endeavors that there is a magical quality to mandalas, an inner knowing that we sense, as if mandalas are a part of our beings. The ability to fully immerse in the creation of a mandala is truly a meditative experience. Viewing the completed work can be breathtaking, while processing the mandala can be revealing and insightful. What better intervention can be used than this?

I truly hope that this book has been both educational and insightful to all who have read it. I hope that the mandala interventions will be utilized, not just in the therapy room, but to enhance your own self-care as well. I wish all of you good health and happiness, and a career filled with joy. Thank you.

References

Armstrong, Stephen. *Sandtray Therapy: A Humanistic Approach*. Ludic Press, 2008.

Arrien, Angeles. *Signs of Life: The Five Universal Shapes and How to Use Them*. Penguin Putnam Inc, 1998.

Art Therapy (2005-2015), *Color Therapy and Healing: An Introduction.* [Online]. [Accessed December, 2014] http://www.arttherapyblog.com.

Art Therapy (2005-2015), *Color Meanings and Symbolism.* [Online]. [Accessed December, 2014] http://www.arttherapyblog.com.

Art Therapy (2005-2015), *Color Psychology: The Emotional Effects of Colors.* [Online]. [Accessed December, 2014] http://www.arttherapyblog.com.

Avalon, Arthur, M.P. Pandit, and Taranatha Vidyaratna. *Kularnava Tantra*. India: Motilal Banarsidass,India, 2007.

Bellantoni, Patti. *If It's Purple, Someone's Gonna Die: The Power of Color in Visual Storytelling*. United States: Elsevier/Focal Press, 2014.

Bryant, Barry, and in cooperation with Namgyal Monastery. *The Wheel of Time Sand Mandala*. [San Francisco, Calif.]: HarperSanFrancisco, 1994.

Buchalter, Susan. *Mandala Symbolism and Techniques*. Jessica Kingsley Pub, 2012.

Chodron, Pema. *Living Beautifully: With Uncertainty and Change*. United States: Shambhala Publications, Inc., 2012.

Crystal Links (1995-2014) *Mandalas.* [Online]. [Accessed November, 2014] http://www.crystallinks.com

Dare to Discern (2005-2015), *Native American Mandala Art Meanings.* [Online}. [Accessed December, 2014] http://www.whats-your-sign.com

Endrass, B., Rehm, M., Andre, E. & Nakano, Y. (2008). *Talk is silver, silence is golden: A cross cultural study on the usage of pauses in speech*. Academic Press.

Fincher, Susanne. *The Mandala Workbook: A Creative Guide for Self-Exploration, Balance, and Well-Being*. Boston & London: Shambhala Publications, Inc., 2009.

Fincher, Susanne, and Robert Johnson. *Creating Mandalas: For Insight, Healing, and Self-Expression*. Boston, Mass: Shambhala Publications Inc, 1992.

Flanagan, Sabina. *Hildegard of Bingen*. Barnes & Noble, 1999.

Fox, Matthew. *Illuminations of Hildegard of Bingen*. Bear & Company, 2003.

Green, Eric, Athena Drewes, and Janice Kominski. (2013). 'Use of Mandalas in Jungian Play Therapy with Adolescents Diagnosed with ADHD.' *International Journal of Play Therapy* 22.3, 159–172.

Gucci, Giuseppe, *The Theory and Practice of the Mandala*, tr. A.H. Broderick, London 1961.

Henderson P., Rosen D, Mascaro N. (2007). 'Empirical Study on the Healing Nature of Mandalas.' *Psychology of Aesthetics, Creativity, and the Arts*, 1.3, 148-154.

Hoeller, Stephan, A. (1989). *The Gnostic Jung and the Seven Sermons to the Dead*, Quest Books.

Homeyer, Linda. *Sandtray Therapy: A Practical Manual*. New York, NY: Taylor & Francis, 2010.

Huyser, Anneke. *Mandala Workbook for Inner Self-Discovery*. Binkey Kok Publications, 2002.

J. Paul Getty Museum (2015), *Understanding Formal Analysis*. [Online]. [Accessed February, 2015] http://www.getty.edu.

Jewish Virtual Library (2015). *Jewish Concepts: Tefillan*. [Online]. [Accessed January, 2015]. http://www.jewishvirtuallibrary.org.

Jung, Carl Gustav G. *Collected Works of C.G. Jung*. London: Routledge & K. Paul, 1974.

Jung, Carl Gustav. *Mandala Symbolism*. Princeton, N.J.]: Princeton University Press, 1992.

Jung, Carl Gustav, *Man and His Symbols*. New York: Doubleday & Company, 1964.

Jung, C., and Michael York. *Memories, Dreams, Reflections*. United States: Shambhala Lion Editions.

Jung, C., and R. Hull. *Psychological Types*. United Kingdom: Routledge, 1992.

Jung, C., and Hull. *Psychology and Western Religion: (From Vols. 11,18 Collected Works)*. Princeton University Press, 1984.

Kellogg, J. (1978). *Mandala: Path of Beauty*. Lightfoot: Mari

Khanna, Madhu. *Yantra: The Tantric Symbol of Cosmic Unity*. Thames & Hudson Ltd, 1979.

Lewis, Richard G. *Color Psychology*. Burbank, CA: Riana Group, 2014.

Malchiodi, Cathy. *The Art Therapy Sourcebook: Art Making for Personal Growth, Insight and Transformation*. Los Angeles: Contemporary Books Inc, 1999.

Malchiodi, Cathy, and Judith Aaron Rubin. *Medical Art Therapy With Children (Art Therapies)*. United Kingdom: JESSICA KINGSLEY PUBLISHERS, United Kingdom, 1999.

McNiff, Shaun. *Art Heals: How Creativity Cures the Soul*. Shambhala Publications, Inc., 2004.

Miller PhD., David. (2005), Mandala Symbolism in Psychotherapy. *The Journal of Transpersonal Psychology*. Volume 37(2), pages 164-177.

Mollica, Patti. *Color Theory*. Quayside Pub Group, 2013.

Morton, Jill. *Color Voodoo #1: A Guide to Color Symbolism*. Colorcom, 2001.

O'Connor, Zena. 'Colour Psychology and Colour Therapy: Caveat Emptor'. *Color Research & Application* 36.3 (2011): 229–234.

Pierce, Kerry M. *Christian Mandalas: Revelation, Reason, Regeneration*. Kerry M. Pierce, 2014.

Religion Facts (2013), *Mandalas: Sacred Art and Geometry*. [Online]. [Accessed December, 2014] http://www.religionfacts.com/buddhism/things/mandalas.htm

Slegelis, Maralynn Hagood. 'A Study of Jung's Mandala and Its Relationship to Art Psychotherapy'. *The Arts in Psychotherapy* 14.4 (1987): 301–311.

Strehlow, Wighard. *Hildegard of Bingen's Spiritual Remedies*. United States: Inner Traditions Bear & Company, 2002.

Tara Mandala (2014), *Buddhist and Native American Practices*. [Online]. [Accessed November, 2014] http//www.taramandala.org.

Ting-Toomey, Stella. *Communicating across Cultures*. 1st ed. New York: Guilford Publications, 1999.

Town, Anne. *Aspects of Colour Through Children's Mandalas*. Anne Town, 2013.

Withrow, R. L. (2004), *The Use of Color in Art Therapy.* The Journal of Humanistic Counseling, Education and Development, 43: 33–40.